citizenship

TODAY

second edition

Collins

chrisculshaw **paul**clarke **neil**reaich **jenny**wales

William Collins' dream of knowledge for all began with the publication of his first book in 1819. A self-educated mill worker, he not only enriched millions of lives, but also founded a flourishing publishing house. Today, staying true to this spirit, Collins books are packed with inspiration, innovation and practical expertise. They place you at the centre of a world of possibility and give you exactly what you need to explore it.

Collins. Do more.

Published by Collins
An imprint of HarperCollinsPublishers
77–85 Fulham Palace Road
Hammersmith
London
W6 8JB

Browse the complete Collins catalogue at
www.collinseducation.com

© HarperCollinsPublishers Limited 2006

10 9 8 7 6 5 4 3 2 1

ISBN-13 978 0 00 722063 2

ISBN-10 0 00 722063 4

Jenny Wales, Chris Culshaw, Paul Clarke and Neil Reaich assert their moral rights to be identified as the authors of this work.

British Library Cataloguing in Publication Data
A Catalogue record for this publication is available from the British Library

This high quality material is endorsed by Edexcel and has been through a rigorous quality assurance programme to ensure that it is a suitable companion to the specification for both learners and teachers. This does not mean that its contents will be used verbatim when setting examinations nor is it to be read as being the official specification – a copy of which is available at www.edexcel.org.uk.

Commissioned by Abigail Woodman
Project editor: Kate Wigley
Picture research: Thelma Gilbert
Cover design: Bluepig Design
Cover image: courtesy of Corbis
Internal design: Aetos Ltd.
Illustrations: Yane Christensen, Sylvie Poggio Artists Agency; Aetos Ltd.
Index: Indexing Specialists (UK) Ltd.
Production: Sarah Robinson
Printed and bound by Martins the Printers Ltd., Berwick-upon-Tweed

Acknowledgements
HarperCollinsPublishers would like to thank the readers of the first edition, Anne Murray-Hudson, David Barrs and Nicholas Price, and Anthony Batchelor, Principal Examiner of Citizenship for Edexcel for his input as Consultant on this project.
We would also like to take this opportunity to thank Trevor Green, Chief Examiner of Citizenship for Edexcel for his comments on the second edition and Chloe Parker of Islington Green School in London for her valuable comments on Theme 2: Power, Politics and the Media. Also, thanks to Jo Swinson, MP for her contribution.
The publishers would like to thank the following for permission to reproduce photographs. The page number is followed, where necessary, by t (top), m (middle), b (bottom), l (left), or r (right).

p.4 (t) Photofusion/Brian Mitchell, (b) Photofusion/Stan Gamester;
p.5 (t) Science Photo Library/Mauro Fermarielle, (b) Topfoto;
p6 (t) Sally & Richard Greenhill, (m) Photofusion/Ulrike Preuss, (b) Still Pictures/Jorgen Schytte; p.8 Photofusion/Christa Stadtler;
p.9 Photofusion/Graham Burns; p.18 (l) Sally & Richard Greenhill, (m) Photofusion, (r) Still Pictures/Hartmut Schwarzbach, (b) Xinhua News Service; p.22 (tl) John Walmsley, (bl) Photofusion/Jacky Chapman; p.24 Rex Features; p.27 Impact Photos; p.28 (tl) Sally & Richard Greenhill, (tm) Rex Features, (tr) Alamy/Domonic Burke, (bl) Alamy/Ruben Abboud, (br) Photofusion/Paul Doyle; p.29 Empics;
p.31 (tl) Photofusion/David Montford, (bl) Getty-Images, (m) Magnum Photos, (r) Photofusion/Ulrike Preuss; p.32 Photofusion/Brian Mitchell; p.33 (l) Empics, (r) Sally & Richard Greenhill; p.34 Campaign for Racial Equality; p.36 (l) Photofusion/Paula Solloway, (r) Magnum Photos; p.37 Still Pictures/Tim Page; p.38 (tl) Corbis/Bettman, (bl) Photofusion/Jackie Chapman, (r) Corbis; p.40 Science Photo Library/Alex Bartell; p.41 Sally & Richard Greenhill; p.42 Photofusion/Christa Stadtler; p.44 (t) Alamy/Jeff Morgan, (b) Popperfoto; p.46 Empics; p.47 Corbis; p.48 (t) Corbis, (b) Sally & Richard Greenhill; p.49 Rex Features; p.50 (t) Empics, (b) Rex Features; p.52 Rex Features; p.53 Rex Features; p.56 (l) Photofusion/Gary Simpson, (r) Photofusion/Paul Baldesare; p.57 Rex Features; p.64 John Walmsley; p.65 Photofusion/Maggie Murray; p.66 Alamy/Buzz Pictures; p.67 (l) Photofusion/Paula Solloway, (r) Rex Features; p.68 Alamy/Buzz Pictures; p.70 (t) Rex Features, (b) Photofusion/Ray Roberts; p.72 Corbis; p.73 Topfoto; p.74 Alamy/Andre Jenny, p.75 (l) Photofusion/Ulrike Preuss, (r) Photofusion/Ulrike Preuss; p.76 (t) Courtesy of Jo Swinson, (b) Empics; p.77 Sally & Richard Greenhill; p.78 Paul Hackett; p.79 Empics; p.80 (l) Alamy/John Powell, (tr) Rex Features, (br) Photofusion/Stan Gamester; p.81 Rex Features; p.82 (tl) Photofusion/Jacky Chapman, (tm) Photofusion/Libby Welsh, (tr) Photofusion, (b) Photofusion/Sally Lancaster; p.84 Coleman & Partners Architects on behalf of Plus Shops Ltd; p.85 Greenpeace; p.86 (l) Getty-Images, (m) Sally & Richard Greenhill, (r) Photofusion/Gary Parker; p.87 Empics; p.88 National Youth Agency; p.89 Rex Features; p90 Popperfoto; p.91 Roger Scruton; p.92 Getty-Images/AFP; p.93 (l) Corbis, (r) Getty-Images/AFP; p.94 (l) Corbis, (m) Rex Features, (r) Rex Features p.96 Alamy; p.98 (t) Getty-Images, (bl) Topfoto, (br) Rex Features; p.100 Corbis; p.110 Getty-Images/Image Bank; p.111 (l) Rex Features, (r) Rex Features; p.113 Alamy; p.114 Empics; p.115 Alamy/Photo Library Wales; p.116 Alamy/Motoring Picture Library; p.117 Photofusion/Ulrike Preuss; p.118 (l) Getty-Images, (tr) Corbis, (br) Alamy/Janine Weidel; p.120 Still Pictures/Jorgen Schytte; p.121 Empics; p.122 Rex Features; p.123 Still Pictures/Mark Edwards; p.124 (t) Rex Features, (b) Still Pictures; p.125 Still Pictures/Hartmut Schwarzbach; p.126 Rex Features; p.127 Corbis; p.128 Still Pictures; p.129 (l) Still Pictures, (r) Village Aid; p.130 Alamy/Jeff Morgan; p.131 Rex Features; p.132 (t) Courtesy of Xerox, (bl) Alamy, (br) Remarkable Pencils; p.133 Alamy/Photofusion; p.135 Photofusion/John Booth; p.136 Empics; p.137 (t) Corbis, (l) Empics, (r) Reuters/Pierre Holtz; p.138 Rex Features; p.140 Alamy/Ace Stock; p.141 Alamy; p.142 Getty-Images/Tom Owen Edmunds; p.144 (t) Still Pictures, (b) Topfoto; p.145 (l) Rex Features, (r) Still Pictures/Hartmut Schwarzbach; p.147 Getty-Images/AFP; p.149 (l) Amnesty International, (r) Greenpeace.

The publishers gratefully acknowledge the following for permission to reproduce copyright material. Every effort has been made to trace copyright holders, but in some cases this has proved impossible. The publishers would be happy to hear from any copyright holder that has not been acknowledged.

Thanks to:
Amnesty International for the article on Aster Yohannes: p. 149;
BBC News website (http://news.bbc.co.uk) for use of 'Cinema complex plans win go-ahead', June 18th 2004: p. 84;
Crown copyright material is reproduced with the permission of the Controller of HMSO and the Queen's Printer for Scotland: p. 25, 26, 27, 28, 40, 71, 76, 91, 98, 101, 134;
Edexcel for the use of questions from the Edexcel GCSE (Short course) in Citizenship Studies papers 2003, 2004 and 2005: p.18, 58–61, 104–107, 150–153;
European Communities, 1995–2005 for the use of statistics: p. 132, 133;
Greenpeace for the use of a letter on their website (www.greenpeace.org): p. 149;
London School of Economics for the use of 'UK Children Go Online', (www.children-go-online.net): p. 100;
Ofcom for the use of 'Interest in television programme type; by age': p99;
Oxford University Press for the use of statistics from the Human Development Report 2005: p. 120, 122;
Population Reference Bureau for use of HIV/AIDS statistics: p. 146;
St Albans Youth Council for the use of their homepage (www.sayc.org.uk): p. 72.

Contents

What is Citizenship ?

1 Look at the pictures on these two pages. Write down the problem that each one shows.

2 What could be done to help overcome each problem?

3 Who do you think should be responsible for solving the problems?

What's involved?

The issues in the pictures cover some of the areas of citizenship that you will work on through the Citizenship Studies GCSE short course. All the images show different aspects of life and suggest ways in which people might find themselves in difficulties, both big and small. For example:

- If the local cinema closes, it may be a pain but there is likely to be another one fairly near.

- If nobody buys the coffee you grow, finding another way of life will be difficult.

- If you use a wheelchair and there are no ramps next to the steps, you will face problems.

- If people are messing up your local environment, who will have to pay the price?

- Laws are passed to try to make life better for everyone, but some people break them.

- You might need a new school or hospital where you live, but the Government may not choose to spend its money that way.

Citizenship is about learning to live together as a community, both within your own country and beyond. Citizenship education gives people the knowledge they need to play a full and active part in society. Understanding how society works will help you to live more easily within it, and give you the power to make things better for other people, too.

Your Citizenship course will help you to understand how you can make your voice heard and change things you don't like. You often hear people say 'They must... ' or 'I can't do anything about it.' You can! Get involved and you'll be surprised.

Your Citizenship Studies course

Your Citizenship Studies course explores citizenship issues, and helps you to understand your role and how you can be involved.

There are two parts to the course:
- Part one is called Participating in Society.
- Part two is called Citizenship Today.

Citizenship Today is divided into three themes:

Theme 1: Human rights

This theme explores different communities in the UK. It shows that respect and understanding between people help to create a better society. You will look at our rights and responsibilities as individuals, consumers and employees. You will also learn why laws are needed and about the kinds of laws that protect citizens.

Theme 2: Power, politics and the media

This theme shows how you can make a change to society, both as an individual and as a member of voluntary groups. A section on political power shows how you can make a difference by voting in elections. You will learn how you can speak to your local council about issues that concern you and how people can get involved in pressure groups. You will also explore the power of the media in today's society.

Theme 3: The global village

This theme shows you how the economy works and how it affects everyone. You will explore the ways in which business affects our lives, both in the UK and in the rest of the world. Other global issues are examined in a section on the environment, which focuses on environmental problems and offers some possible solutions. You will learn about some international organizations, such as the European Union and the United Nations, and find out what they do. Finally, you will read about international pressure groups such as Amnesty International, and discover how you can contribute to their work.

The assessment

The assessment has two parts to match the two parts of the course:

- a Citizenship Activity portfolio (Participating in Society)
- a written exam (Citizenship Today).

Part one: the Citizenship Activity

Participating in Society
Internal assessment portfolio
40% of total marks

You take part in a **Citizenship Activity**. As well as doing the activity, you have to:

- describe how you planned the activity
- write about how you carried it out
- provide evidence of your activity and how you went about it
- describe how well you thought it went and whether you think it was a useful Citizenship Activity.

When you hand in your portfolio, it needs to contain:

- a **front sheet** saying what the activity is
- a four-page **response form** with these sections:
  - **Section one**: Planning
  - **Section two**: Activity log
  - **Section three**: Communication with supporting evidence
  - **Section four**: Evaluation.

  Planning and Evaluation don't have to be written. You can do a spoken presentation of these two sections, but you must be able to prove that you did the presentation.

Part two: the written exam

Edexcel Citizenship Today
Written paper
1 hour 30 minutes   60% of total marks

Section A	This examines your **Citizenship Activity**. You will: • answer short-answer questions about your Citizenship Activity • write a long answer about your Citizenship Activity.
Section B	This examines your knowledge, understanding and ability to interpret information on one of the three themes. You will: • be given a variety of information sources, e.g. short texts, graphs and pictures to do with **ONE** of the themes from the content • answer short-answer questions about the information you have been given.
Section C	This examines your knowledge, understanding and ability to interpret information across the three themes. You will: • answer short-answer questions on **ALL** the themes from the content • write a long answer to **ONE** question, which you can choose from **ONE** of the themes.

Pages 8–15 show you how to carry out your Citizenship Activity for **Participating in Society**.

Pages 16–19 show you in more detail what the written exam for **Citizenship Today** includes, and how to answer the questions.

The Citizenship Activity: what can you do?

The activity

Your Citizenship Studies course requires you to take part in a Citizenship Activity, keep a record of how it works and decide how well it went. You may already be involved in suitable activities, but if not, you'll need to choose what to do. There are many possibilties for you to consider.

- Is there an open space that could be turned into a garden or other sort of community or school resource?
- Are there older people who would enjoy a regular visit?
- Can you help some younger people with their reading?
- Can you work with other young people to discuss community issues such as graffiti, vandalism or services that you would like to see in your area?
- Can you carry out a Citizenship-based project while on work experience (e.g. finding out about health and safety in the work place)?
- Do you have a school council? If not, could you set one up?

- Could you organize a school event, perhaps to raise money for a good cause?
- Could you find out about employment rights and responsibilities when you do your work experience?
- Does your school have a radio station? If not, could you start one up?
- Could you run a mock election or trial, or hold a meeting for an international organization?
- Could you organize a petition, opinion poll or display about something you care about, such as an environmental issue?
- Could you run a mini-enterprise?

Your activity could be based on any of these ideas. Remember that being involved in something that really interests you always makes the task easier. For example, does the environment concern you? Are you worried about crime in your area? Or do you want more facilities for young people in the area?

If your activity is based on work experience, you will need to think carefully about what you want to find out. How about rights and responsibilities of people in the workplace? Or could you investigate how the business is affected by consumer protection laws?

If you are making things or providing a service, such as providing refreshments at the school fair, you might be able to turn it into a mini-enterprise. This would mean deciding on the costs of all the things you need and thinking about the price you can charge. You would need to do some research into this. How will you market your product? How much profit do you aim to make? How will you use the profits to benefit your school or community?

The right choice

The one really important thing to remember is that your activity must fit into the Citizenship Studies specification. If you run a cake sale, or a five-a-side football match, for example, you must know why you are doing it and understand the benefits that result from it. Your reasoning must appear in your response form. The emphasis should always be on working with others and on participation.

Working in a team

The Citizenship Activity requires you to work as part of a team. The team may be made up of your school friends or it may be a group outside school. It is important to think about the contribution each person makes to the activity. Make sure that everyone has a role in the activity; it makes it much easier to identify each person's contribution if you can explain their area of responsibility.

A group of students clears a corner of the school grounds to create a garden.

1 Make a list of the contributions you think people will have to make to plan and carry out this activity.

2 Why do you think it is a good activity for Citizenship Studies?

3 Which part of the course does it relate to? See page 6.

Take action

Sit down with a blank sheet of paper and think about what Citizenship Activity you want to do.

1 Start by writing down all your ideas.
2 List all the advantages and disadvantages of each idea.
3 Put them in order from best to worst.
4 Is the one at the top the one you really want to carry out? If so, go ahead. If not, have another look at the list.

Check point

Before you make a final decision, check with your teacher that your activity is suitable for the exam requirements.

In both the exam and the response form in your portfolio, you will need to describe and analyse the contribution you and the others in your group made to the Citizenship Activity. So it's a good idea to think about this right from the start of your activity.

The Citizenship Activity: planning

The steps to success

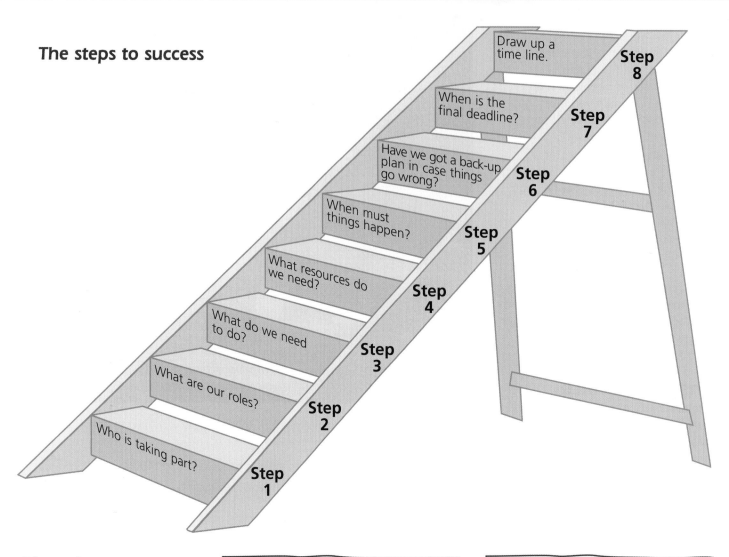

Draw up a time line. **Step 8**

When is the final deadline? **Step 7**

Have we got a back-up plan in case things go wrong? **Step 6**

When must things happen? **Step 5**

What resources do we need? **Step 4**

What do we need to do? **Step 3**

What are our roles? **Step 2**

Who is taking part? **Step 1**

Planning

Planning means setting out what must be done and making sure that everyone knows their responsibilities. By following the steps above, you will be on the right track. You will need to put together two documents:

A list of group members and their responsibilities.

Brainstorm all the things that need to be done. Can you divide these things easily into groups? Who has the skills needed for each activity? Should people work in pairs or on their own?

Then, when you have made these decisions, draw up a list to explain exactly what everyone has to do.

Make sure you keep the list safe. You will need it to check whether everything has been done and to put in your records.

A time line showing what must be done and when.

Using the information you have gathered for your first document, draw up your time line and put the name of the person responsible beside every point.

This will give you markers to check whether everything is on track. It will also give everyone target dates for getting things done.

Remember that gathering information can take time, so make it a priority.

Example: A mini-enterprise making things for the school fair

October 1
Set up enterprise
Allocate roles
Decide on the product
Decide on materials needed
Find suppliers and prices of materials

October 7
Work out costs
Work out expected price
Order supplies
Think about marketing

October 21
Start production
Plan marketing

November 7
Start marketing

November 28
School fair
Sell products
Collect revenue from sales

December 3
Present financial information
Work out amount of money to be given to charity

Take action

When you have decided on your activity, get together with the rest of the team and work out how you are going to go about planning and putting your ideas into action.

Check point

Response form
Section one: Planning

You need to show how you planned your activity in Section one of your response form. You can use your two documents, the 'List of group members and their responsibilities' and the 'Time line', to show this.

You can also describe how you planned the activity by doing a presentation. If you do this, you will need to provide evidence that you made the presentation. You could use any transparencies or PowerPoint slides from your presentation or statements from people who heard your presentation.

The Citizenship Activity: gathering the evidence

1 How are these students showing their citizenship skills?
2 What do you think they had to do to plan this activity?
3 What sort of evidence do you think they collected for their portfolio?
4 How does their activity relate to the content of the course?

Keeping track

While you are carrying out your Citizenship Activity, you need to keep careful records of everything you do. This will include an **activity log** and a collection of **supporting evidence**. They will build a picture both of what you did and of how you did it. Gathering all the information as you go along will help you to put it all together. It's very easy to forget exactly what happened and when!

Keeping an activity log

In the activity log, you will record everything you take part in, such as meetings, research, presentations, or anything else that contributes to your activity. At each stage, you should explain what you are trying to achieve. If you have changed your plans at any point, these changes should be included and explained. You should also record who else was involved in each event and when it took place. There is also a space in which you MUST explain how your activity fits into the Citizenship Studies specification.

Activity Log		
Activity Log	**Group/individual**	**Date**
Meeting with teacher at local primary school to discuss arrangements for giving reading support to Year 2 children. Programme set to start from 22 Jan. Ms Osborne gave guidance on helping with reading.	Ms Ann Osborne (teacher) Paul West Suzanna Giuliani Rajesh Golcha Kate Ridley	8 Jan
Team meeting to discuss plans and share ideas on working with the children.	Paul West Suzanna Giuliani Rajesh Golcha Kate Ridley	15 Jan
First session with children. The team each worked with three children. Ms Osborne gave feedback to help next time.	Ms Ann Osborne Paul West Suzanna Giuliani Rajesh Golcha Kate Ridley	22 Jan

Supporting evidence

There are all sorts of ways in which you can submit your supporting evidence. It doesn't just have to be in writing. You need to provide between one and four pieces of evidence. Just submitting an agenda for a meeting isn't really enough. You would need some other evidence as well. If the work is all written, it should be between 500 and 1000 words. There are all sorts of ways of recording your activity. Here are some suggestions:

- PowerPoint slides
- videos
- CD-Roms
- letters
- photographs
- banners
- web pages
- audio or written records of presentation work
- extended written work
- questionnaires
- agendas or minutes of meetings.

A video that showed the extent of your activity would be fine. An audio recording of a meeting or a presentation about carrying out your activity would also give a clear picture of how you were working. If you use PowerPoint or some other presentation software to explain or persuade people of your point of view, that will make a good piece of evidence. If you create a website to let people know your plans, this will be helpful evidence as it shows just what you were trying to do and how you went about it. If you investigate what people want or think, you may use a questionnaire. This, together with the results, would make a good piece of evidence as it would show the way you worked and what you found out. You might write a document to explain, persuade or justify what you are planning. This would also be a useful piece of supporting evidence, as it would give people a good picture of the activity.

Check point

Response form

Section two: Activity log

You need to include the activity log in Section two of your response form. It should show how the activity relates to issues covered in the content of the course. You should include details of how individuals, and the group as a whole, contributed to the activity.

Check point

Response form

Section three: Communication with supporting evidence

For this section of the response form, you have to list all the materials and sources you have used as your supporting evidence. You should describe how each piece of evidence helped you do the activity. For example, an agenda of a meeting helped you plan a particular stage of your activity, or a questionnaire helped you get information about your activity. It is also very important that you show how the evidence you have gathered can be used to support arguments and make judgements.

The Citizenship Activity: evaluation

Did you make a difference?

When your activity has been completed, there are just two things left to do:

1 **Weigh up your contribution**

    Look back at everything you did. Did you have a leadership role? Did you help to keep people on track? Were you are good team member? Did you have an effect on outsiders? Did you suggest changes in the plan? Would you have done anything differently? How do you think others viewed your contribution? Could you have done more?

2 **Weigh up the contribution of others**

    Who were the main contributors? How did they contribute? Were they good team members? Were some people more important than others? Why? Did one person have an effect on others? Were there difficult moments or low points?

Your answers to the questions above will depend on the sort of activity you took part in. For example:

- if your group was involved in helping younger children with their reading, did you feel they enjoyed it and that you helped their reading to progress?
- if your group ran a mini-enterprise, did you make sure people didn't spend too much on making the product?
- if your group was trying to persuade the local council to provide more sports facilities, did you manage to get a report in the local paper or on local radio?
- would you do things differently another time?
- how effectively did your activity fit into the content of the Citizenship Studies specification?

Summary of Participating in Society

Your portfolio needs to contain:

- a front sheet describing the activity
- a four-page response form with these sections:
  - Section one: Planning
  - Section two: Activity log
  - Section three: Communication with supporting evidence
  - Section four: Evaluation.

Planning and Evaluation don't have to be written. You can do a spoken presentation of these sections, but you must be able to prove that you did the presentation.

Your teacher will give you the response form to fill in. There isn't a lot of space on it, so keep your thoughts simple and straightforward. You will probably want to write it in rough before you fill it in.

At the end of the course

When you have completed your Citizenship Activity, make sure you don't forget about what you did. Section A of the exam is based on your Citizenship Activity. First of all, you will be asked to review the work you have done in your activity. Then you will be posed a question that relates your activity to the rest of the Citizenship course. More information on section A of the exam can be found on page 17.

Check point

Response form

Section four: Evaluation

This is the last section of the response form. This is where you write up your thoughts about everybody's contribution to the activity and say how successful you thought it was. Was there any point at which you could have done things differently? Could you have done things better? If you prefer, you can do a spoken presentation of your evaluation of the activity, but you must provide supporting evidence that you have done it.

The exam: getting it right

What's it all about?

The Citizenship Studies exam is all about being able to use the knowledge you have learnt during the course. The exam paper is full of prompts and stories to help you. You have to apply your knowledge and understanding to be able to answer the questions and draw conclusions.

There are three sections in the exam. They aim to test the knowledge and skills you have developed as well as assessing how you participated in your Citizenship Activity.

Section A asks you about your Citizenship Activity, so you need to remember what you did and how it worked. It also asks you to think about how it related to your citizenship knowledge and skills you have learnt during the course. Many students really shine in this section. The Citizenship Activity is often fun to do, so you remember it very well. You also have a copy of the internal assessment portfolio that contributes to your exam, so revision is easy.

Section B is based on one of the three themes of the specification:

Theme 1 Human Rights	Theme 2 Power, politics and the media	Theme 3 The global village
Communities and identities	Power and politics	Global business
Roles, rights and responsibilities		Environmental issues
Criminal and civil justice	The media	The United Kingdom's place in the world

The questions are all based on evidence about different aspects of one of these themes.

Section C has two parts. The first part contains some short answer questions on all three of the themes. The second part asks you to choose a longer piece of writing about one of the themes. What's really important in the longer piece of writing is to argue more than one point of view. Citizenship Studies is about understanding other people's points of view, so this is your opportunity to show your skills.

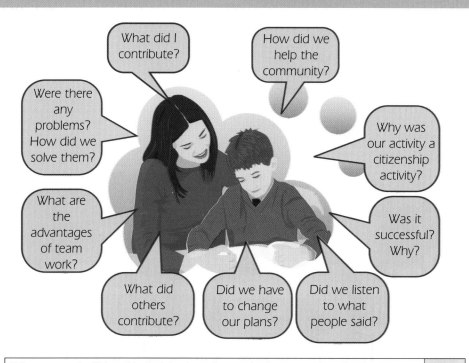

Speech bubbles around the students:
- What did I contribute?
- How did we help the community?
- Were there any problems? How did we solve them?
- Why was our activity a citizenship activity?
- What are the advantages of team work?
- Was it successful? Why?
- What did others contribute?
- Did we have to change our plans?
- Did we listen to what people said?

Section A: answering the questions

Section A is made up of two sorts of questions:

1 **Short answer questions worth one or two marks for each part of the question.**

There are plenty of ideas surrounding the student in the picture. Think about what your answers would be to each of them and you'll have made a good start for the exam.

2 **A longer question worth eight marks.**

You are given a statement and asked if you agree with this point of view (see example below). The most important thing is to show that you have considered another point of view. If you don't, you can only get half marks. So have a look at the exam question and work out your two points of view. There are bullet points after the question to help you with your answer. Don't just repeat them: try to include the answers to them in your writing.

	Leave margin blank
"The success of a Citizenship Activity depends on enthusiasm more than planning." Do you agree with this view? Think about the successes and difficulties you and others experienced during your Citizenship Activity. Give reasons for your opinion, showing you have considered another point of view. You should include the following points in your answer and other information of your own. <ul><li>What makes us feel enthusiastic about an activity?</li><li>Why do we need planning or co-ordination?</li><li>Could the activity succeed without organization?</li><li>What would an activity be like if it were based on enthusiasm rather than planning?</li></ul>	

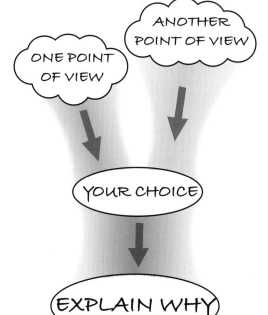

ANOTHER POINT OF VIEW
ONE POINT OF VIEW
YOUR CHOICE
EXPLAIN WHY

Take action

Check that you have a copy of your completed response form and any other material that you used before you hand it to your teacher.

When you have completed your activity, have a look at the questions on this page and some past exam papers. Work out how you would answer the questions using your Citizenship Activity as an example, just as you will do in the exam.

Check point

Thinking about the questions will also help you to complete your activity log. It's more than just a diary of events. It helps you to work out why your activity is a Citizenship Activity by asking you to think about how it contributes to the community. Remember to show how it relates to the content of the Citizenship Studies specification.

The exam: know it, use it

Sections B and C: what sort of questions?

Sections B and C of the exam paper are based on the three themes in the specification represented by the pictures above. You need to know about all three themes because there are questions on all of them. This book follows the specification exactly, so it shows you exactly what you need to know. At the end of each theme, you will find real Edexcel exam questions, with answers and helpful tips on how to score the best marks.

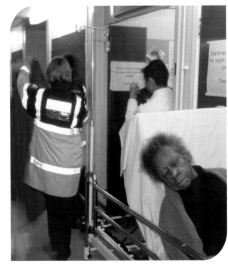
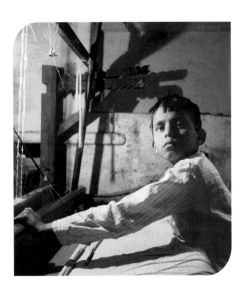

Evidence-based questions

All four questions in **Section B** are based on current evidence. This might be presented as words, numbers or photographs. Each year one of the themes is chosen for this section.

Evidence in the exam

Railway crime

Reported offences	Total number	Changes in the number	Percentage change
Endangering safety	885	+470	+53%
Obstructions	1,302	+600	+46·1%

Jail for truant's mother

When rights and responsibilities clash....

Is the government about to save thousands of lives by banning smoking at work? Anti-smoking campaigners claim the government has not done this yet because it fears a ban will prove too expensive for bars, clubs and hotels. The total savings to the government and businesses, including the NHS, could be £21 billion.

Source: Edexcel Citizenship Studies 2003, 2004, 2005

Introduction

Within each question, you will find a range of short questions worth between one and four marks.

If there's one mark, you only need to give one response. Don't do more; you are only wasting time. If there are two marks, the question will tell you clearly how to earn them. For example:

- **Name** the organization the soldiers in the picture are representing.
- **Identify** and explain two ways in which people found guilty of this offence might be dealt with by the courts.
- **State** two different responsibilities…

Short answer questions

At the beginning of **Section C**, you will find a series of short answer questions. They range across all three themes, so you may be expected to know about all sorts of things from the specification. The questions might be on issues such as:

- human rights
- what identity means
- how Parliament works
- why people should vote in elections
- the work of the EU or the UN
- fair trade.

These are just a few suggestions. You can pick up marks in this section just by knowing the content of the specification.

Some questions have four marks so there is a bit more work to do! For example:

- "Television and radio are much less biased than newspapers."

Identify and explain two reasons why this might be true. Here you will get one mark for each reason you write down and another mark for each explanation. Don't give more than two reasons and two explanations. There are only four marks, so if you do more you will be wasting time.

Longer writing

The final section of the exam gives you some choice. You can pick the theme you want to write about. The format of these questions is just like the long question about your Citizenship Activity (see page 17). The most important things to remember are that:

- you will only get half marks if you argue only from one point of view
- you should use the bullet pointed questions to help you develop your answer. Don't just repeat them, but try to include the answers to them in your writing.

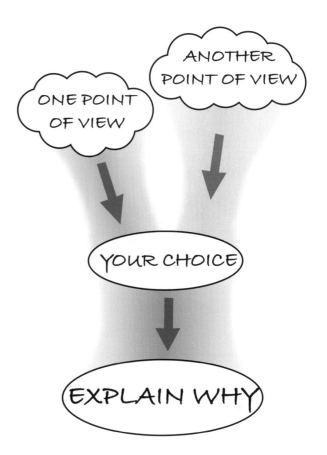

ONE POINT OF VIEW

ANOTHER POINT OF VIEW

YOUR CHOICE

EXPLAIN WHY

Take action

Keep up to date with what's in the news. Much of the exam is based on current events.

Practise looking at issues from other people's point of view. When you see a story on the TV or in the newspapers, think about how people with opposing views see the issue.

Check point

As you work through the book:

- use the **Key Terms** on each page to help you build up your knowledge.
- go through the questions in **Check your understanding** so that you can explain your knowledge.

Theme 1

Human

rights

What is a community?

Getting you thinking

1 How many of these communities do you belong to?

2 How many of these communities do you share with people of different ages and/or interests?

3 If you don't belong to some of these communities, do you know people who do? How do you know these people?

4 What do these communities give you and what do you give them?

Belonging to a community

A **community** is a group of people who are connected in some way. Most people belong to several communities. Someone your age, living in the UK, could be a member of all these communities: school, the local neighbourhood, the country, the European Union, a religious group and others.

Neighbourhoods

There is a lot of overlap between different communities.

A **neighbourhood** community refers to those people who share local interests because of where they live.

It might be the whole of a village or small town, but in a city the neighbourhood can be more difficult to identify. For example, someone living in Whitechapel in London might think of the neighbourhood as 'London', 'Whitechapel', 'the East End' or even just their own particular street.

'I belong to … '

As well as belonging to a neigbourhood, people are also connected by their lifestyle, religion, ethnicity or nationality.

You will discover the meaning of community and understand how you can belong to more than one community at the same time.

The Chinese community

The Chinese community in the UK dates back to the mid-1800s. They live in all parts of the UK and there are well established 'Chinatowns' in Birmingham, Liverpool, London, Manchester and Newcastle. There are over 400 Chinese organizations that serve the needs of the Chinese community in the UK, including language schools, women's groups, and art and business associations. Chinese New Year, food, martial arts, medicine and Feng Shui have all become part of British life.

The Christian community

There are almost 49 000 Christian churches in the United Kingdom across more than ten different denominations, ranging from Church of England and Roman Catholic to Methodist and Greek Orthodox. As well as involving people in the wider Christian community, many churches are a focus for local people, offering facilities and events open to Christians and non-Christians alike.

Irish travellers

There are about 1300 Irish travellers in Northern Ireland. They are a centuries-old ethnic community that travels around in mobile homes. They have their own culture, customs, traditions and language.

The Muslim community

Almost all of the Muslim population in Britain are descendants of the families of people who came to Britain in the 1950s, 60s and 70s. However, Islam has been followed in Britain for centuries. At least 300 years ago, Indian-Muslim sailors, recruited by the East India Company, settled in port towns. The first mosque in Britain probably opened in Cardiff in 1860. Today, there are Muslim communities all over Britain.

Check your understanding

1 Explain why people can belong to more than one community and why there is an overlap between communities.
2 Describe what each of the communities shown has in common. What makes each one a community?

What's your opinion?

'It is easier to feel part of a community if you live in a village or small town rather than a city.'
Do you agree with this statement? Give reasons for your opinion, showing you have considered another point of view.

Key Terms

community: a group of people who are in close contact and who share common interests and values

neighbourhood: a local area within which people live as neighbours, sharing living space and interests

A national culture

Getting you thinking

These images are all associated with British culture. What other images would you add?

What does it mean to be British?

This is a difficult question and it has many possible answers. Do you think it means that:

- you share a geographical boundary with other British people?
- you share a history that links the separate parts of England, Wales, Scotland and Northern Ireland?
- you share a common language?
- you identify with many common habits, values and pastimes?
- you have the right to have a British passport so you can move freely in and out of the United Kingdom?

A national identity is often easier to describe when you are in a different country. How might you feel if you went abroad on holiday? In Spain, for example, you would come across a different language, a different kind of diet, different kinds of schooling and different games played by children and adults.

A sense of belonging

A sense of belonging comes from growing up and living in a particular place. Parents, schools and the media pass on common ideas of British culture. Different generations are also influenced by their own personal experiences. People who have fought in wars for their country are likely to feel a different sense of belonging from those who only feel British when they are away on holiday.

Which community?

People may also identify with different kinds of national community. People from ethnic minorities may feel more comfortable with members of their own ethnic community than with other **British nationals**. Similarly, people from various regions such as the Midlands or the South West might identify more with people from their own region than with people from other regions.

It is possible to belong to many different communities at the same time. Sports fans may feel quite comfortable supporting a British team in one competition, an English or Welsh team in another, and their local team in a third.

You will explore the meaning of national identity and culture, and discover that Britain is a multicultural country.

A multicultural community

Population of Great Britain by ethnic group (millions)

White	52.5
Black Caribbean	0·5
Black African	0·4
Indian	1·0
Pakistani	0·7
Bangladeshi	0·3
Chinese	0·2
Other groups	2·0

Source: Social Trends 2005, ONS

The ethnic mix of the national community has changed steadily over the years to include a significant number of people of Afro-Caribbean, African and Asian descent. In some areas, the majority of the local population is now of one of these groups. Many of them have developed a sense of belonging and feel British, as the graph on the right shows.

In a **multicultural community**:

- a local school may serve a community with several different home languages and different festivals to celebrate
- welfare services often provide information printed in several languages
- hospitals and clinics work with a variety of traditions and expectations surrounding births and deaths
- local councils have to take account of different community needs for shops and religious buildings
- businesses may have staff and customers from a range of cultural backgrounds.

Who feels British?

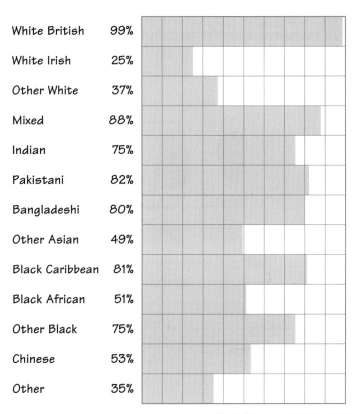

White British	99%
White Irish	25%
Other White	37%
Mixed	88%
Indian	75%
Pakistani	82%
Bangladeshi	80%
Other Asian	49%
Black Caribbean	81%
Black African	51%
Other Black	75%
Chinese	53%
Other	35%

Source: Social Trends 2005, ONS

Action

What do your friends and family mean by 'being British'? Share your findings with the class.

Check your understanding

1 What does it mean to say that Britain is a multicultural community?
2 List as many different aspects of British culture as you can that you think help define British national identity.

What's your opinion?

'The region I live in is more important to me than my national culture.' Do you agree with this statement? Give reasons for your opinion, showing you have considered another point of view.

Key Terms

British nationals: citizens of the United Kingdom

multicultural community: a community made up of people from many different cultural or ethnic groups

Where are your roots?

Getting you thinking

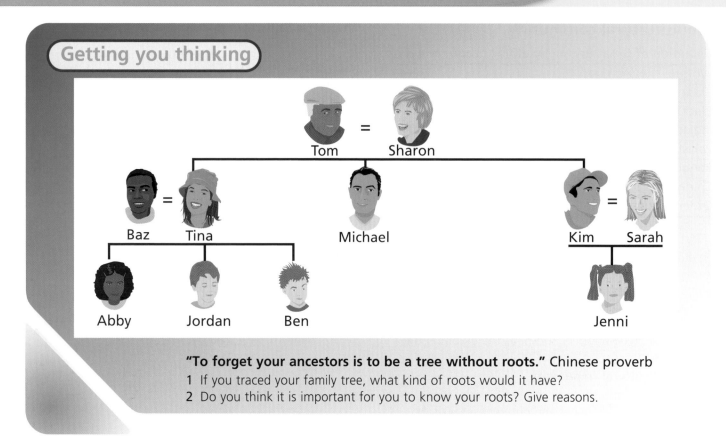

"To forget your ancestors is to be a tree without roots." Chinese proverb

1 If you traced your family tree, what kind of roots would it have?
2 Do you think it is important for you to know your roots? Give reasons.

A pick-and-mix people

Throughout its history, people have settled in Britain from many different countries. They bring their language, ideas and customs, all of which have mixed together to make up the country's culture.

Warlike invasions of Romans, Saxons, Vikings and Normans were followed by peaceful migrations from Europe and many former British colonies. Just look in the dictionary, phone book or map to find words and names from many languages.

In the past 250 years, about six million people have come from Ireland in search of a better life. Many came to the UK during the potato famine of the 1840s.

In 1860, one-quarter of the population of Liverpool were Irish migrants.

Poles have lived here ever since the reign of Queen Elizabeth I, but the majority of UK Poles settled here after World War II when Poland was occupied first by the Nazis, and then by the Soviet armies.

There has been a Jewish population in the UK for hundreds of years, but most arrived in the 1930s and 40s. They came to the UK to escape from religious and racial persecution in Russia and Europe.

In the 1950s, many people from British colonies in Africa, Asia and the Caribbean settled in the UK looking

for work, as there was a shortage of manual and semiskilled employees in Britain during this period.

In the 1970s, thousands of Ugandan Asians arrived here after being expelled from Uganda.

Today **immigration** is more restricted.

In the same way that people from other countries come to Britain, people **emigrate** from Britain to go and live in other countries. The table below shows some reasons for immigration and emigration in Britain.

Why do people come and go? (thousands)			
	Immigration	Emigration	Balance
For work	103·4	92·8	10·6
With a partner	77·2	51·1	26·1
For study	91·2	13·7	77·5
Other	164·6	99·3	65·3
No reason	27·7	49·2	-21·5
All reasons	464·0	306·0	158·0

Source: Social Trends 2005, ONS

You will find out about the diverse communities that make up the UK.

Ethnic minorities in each region

UK average 7%

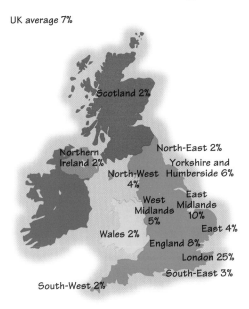

Scotland 2%

Northern Ireland 2%

North-East 2%

Yorkshire and Humberside 6%

North-West 4%

West Midlands 5%

East Midlands 10%

East 4%

Wales 2%

England 8%

London 25%

South-East 3%

South-West 2%

Source: 2001 Census, ONS

Leicester: a lesson in racial understanding

Many people living in Leicester have non-white roots, and Leicester is proud of its **cultural diversity**. However, in the 1970s, it was labelled one of the most racist cities in Britain. There were adverts in the local papers telling immigrants not to come to Leicester and racial tension was high.

The city council took the lead by outlawing racism. It promoted Leicester as a city that welcomes everybody. The council created Britain's first-ever race relations committee. A public education programme made people aware of others' hopes and fears. Since then, various groups have worked hard to promote good race relations in the city.

There are now over 1500 Asian businesses in the city, and many Asian councillors on the city council. Festivals such as Diwali now attract over 25 000 people to the city.

Action

Research the background and culture of any immigrant groups that have settled in your local area. Find out why they left their homelands, and to what extent they have been able to retain their language and culture. Present your findings to the class.

Check your understanding

1 Suggest two reasons why the UK is a culturally diverse society.
2 Why did many immigrants come to Britain in the 1950s?
3 Why do people immigrate and emigrate?
4 In which regions, outside London, would you find the most culturally diverse communities?
5 Describe two things the council did to improve race relations in Leicester.
6 Do you think other regions of the UK will become more culturally diverse in future? Give reasons.

What's your opinion?

'Immigration benefits a country.'
Do you agree with this statement? Give reasons for your opinion, showing you have considered another point of view.

Key Terms

cultural diversity: the range of different groups that make up a wider population

emigration: leaving your homeland to live in another country

immigration: moving to another country to live there

Religious understanding

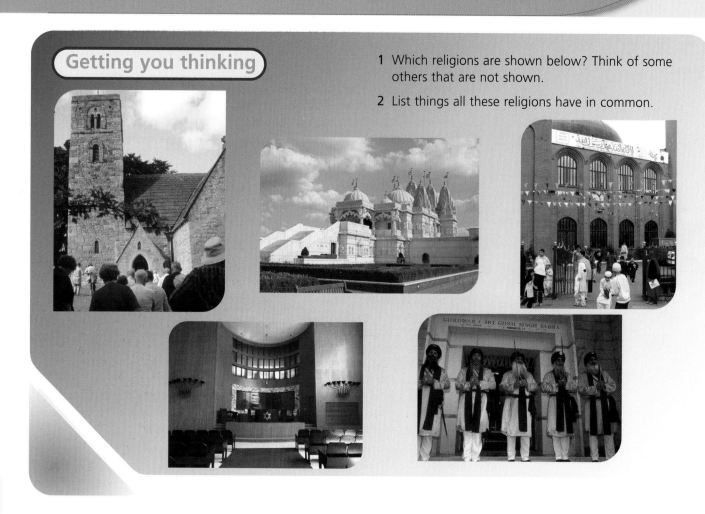

Getting you thinking

1 Which religions are shown below? Think of some others that are not shown.

2 List things all these religions have in common.

Diverse views

Although most UK citizens would probably claim to be Christians, there are many other diverse religious groups in the UK. The majority of these are found in large cities, such as London, Birmingham, Manchester and Leeds, where most of the UK's ethnic **minority** communities live. This religious diversity is the result of people settling here over many years, mostly from former British colonies.

The main ethnic minority groups and their religions are:

- *Bangladeshis*: Mostly Muslim (small number of Hindus)
- *Indians (Punjabis)*: Mostly Sikh, some Hindus
- *Indians (Gujeratis)*: Mostly Hindus, some Muslims
- *Pakistanis*: Muslim
- *Chinese*: Christian, Confucian and Buddhist
- *Afro-Caribbeans*: Christian and Rastafarian.

Within many religions there are different 'branches'. Anglicans, Methodists, Quakers and Catholics are all part of the wider Christian tradition but practise their religion in different ways. In the same way, Orthodox and Reform Jews share many beliefs but worship in separate synagogues.

Sometimes an individual's clothes, the food they eat or the language they speak gives you a clue to their religion. But this is not always the case. Think about all the UK citizens with Indian roots. Some of them are Sikhs, but what about the others?

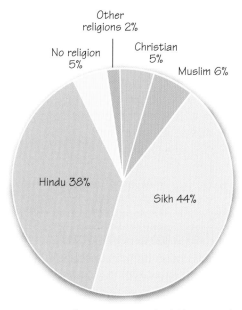

UK citizens with Indian roots: different religions

Other religions 2%
No religion 5%
Christian 5%
Muslim 6%
Hindu 38%
Sikh 44%

Source: www.statistics.gov.uk

Theme 1: Human rights

You will find out about the religious diversity of the UK and why religious tolerance is important.

Religion in conflict

All we wanted was to get our kids to school

3 September, Belfast

Hundreds of riot police and armed soldiers lined the road. They stood between the Protestants, who were shouting threats and abuse, and the Catholic girls and their parents. The girls, aged four to eleven, were on their way to Holy Cross school, a Catholic school in the middle of a Protestant housing estate. A mother of a six-year-old girl said, "It was terrifying. They were shouting 'Dirty tramps. Your kids are animals.' It was like walking into a wall of hate. I didn't think there was so much hate."
At the end of the school day, the girls left the school by a rear entrance and were taken home in taxis.

Asian youths attack church

6 November, Bradford
Police are looking for a gang of Asian youths who tried to set fire to a church on Bonfire Night. When the vicar chased the youths away, they stoned his car. After the police arrived, the youths ran off. After this happened, local Muslims went to a service at the church and, at the end, they spoke to the congregation to express their 'deep regrets'. Also, a joint Christian/Muslim fund-raising group has been set up to raise money for people in Afghanistan.

What do the Holy Cross incident and Bradford attack have in common? What differences are there?

Check your understanding

1 Why does the UK have such a diversity of religions? Can you name any other countries where you find the same religious diversity?
2 What does the Universal Declaration of Human Rights say about your religious freedom? Is this always observed?

What's your opinion?

'It is always important to be **tolerant** of other people's religious beliefs.' Do you agree with this statement? Give reasons for your opinion, showing you have considered another point of view.

Everyone's right

The United Nations (UN), an international organization to which most countries belong, put together a Declaration of Human Rights (see pages 36–37). This Declaration includes a section on religion, which means that everyone is free to follow any religion or to choose to follow none. You have the right to join an established religion, or to start a sect or cult of your own. Nobody should be prevented from following a religion of their choice.

Key Terms

minority: a small part of a larger group of people
tolerant: open-minded, accepting

1.1: Communities and identities

29

Identities

Getting you thinking

I've got Asian roots. I love sport, have loads of mates and I'm always having fun.

I come from Brighton. My parents are divorced. I've got one brother and two half-sisters. I like watching TV and listening to music. I spend loads of time at the beach with my friends.

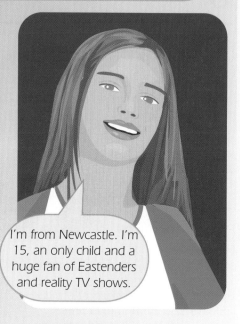

I'm from Newcastle. I'm 15, an only child and a huge fan of Eastenders and reality TV shows.

1 What has contributed to the identity of each of these people?
2 How do you think these factors have affected them?
3 How much does your identity depend on where you live, on your family's roots or on your religion?

4 If you had been asked the question, "Who are you?" when you were five years old, what would you have said? How would you answer this question now?
5 Make a list of factors that will shape your identity as you get older.

Who am I?

In some countries, such as France, all citizens must carry an **identity card**. This card gives details such as name, address and date of birth. But the word '**identity**' has another, broader meaning. The identity of a person is a combination of where they come from and the influences on their life.

Your identity develops and changes as you develop and change. Can you remember how you felt when you first went to school? You've learned a lot about yourself in the ten or more years since then. You now have a better

understanding of your good and bad points; you are more self-aware and better aware of how other people see you. Looking back, that five-year-old 'you' will seem like a very different person. Your identity will continue to develop further as you grow older and as you become an employee, a parent, partner/wife/husband and so on.

An identity card obviously can't show all this information about you. However, some governments like them to be used because it means that people can be easily identified.

You will discover the meaning of identity and some of the factors which determine it.

Conflicting loyalties

Britain has one of the highest rates of mixed-race (**dual heritage**) relationships in the world. By 2010, it is estimated that London will be made up of more dual heritage and black people than white. Whilst most people would agree that cultural diversity is a good thing, the mixing of races and nationalities can occasionally produce conflicts.

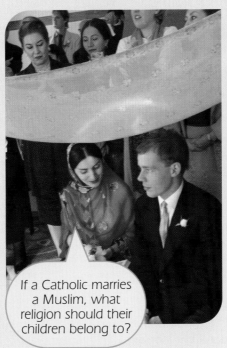

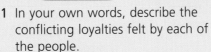

> If, for example, your mother is Chinese, your father is Irish, you were born in Paris but you live in London, how would you answer the question: "Where are you from?"

> If your mother is German and your father is English, who should you support in the World Cup?

> If a Catholic marries a Muslim, what religion should their children belong to?

> How do you react if someone tells you you're not really black and you're not really white?

1 In your own words, describe the conflicting loyalties felt by each of the people.

2 Which person has the most difficult situation to resolve, and why?

3 Suggest other situations which involve conflicting loyalties.

Check your understanding

What does 'dual heritage' mean? Describe how dual heritage can sometimes lead to conflicts of identity.

What's your opinion?

'People are more alike than different.'
Do you agree with this statement? Give reasons for your opinion showing you have considered another point of view.

Key Terms

dual heritage: people with parents or ancestors of different origins

identity: who or what someone or something is

identity card: a card that establishes someone's identity

Meeting barriers

Getting you thinking

Some children were playing on the beach when an old 'bag lady' came along. She was talking to herself and picking things up off the beach as she walked. Parents called their children over and told them stay close by, until the old woman had moved on. The following day, they discovered that the old woman came to the beach every day, picking up bits of glass so children wouldn't cut their feet.

1 Why did the parents call their children over? What is the moral of the story?

2 Have you ever misjudged somebody because of their dress or behaviour? Have you ever been misjudged?

3 Think of individuals or groups who are misjudged in this way, and say why they have been misunderstood.

Prejudice and discrimination

People treat each other badly for all sorts of reasons. Such unfair treatment can mean that people don't get jobs or are kept out of clubs, as well as many other things. The case studies on the next page show some strategies used to overcome prejudice and discrimination.

The pyramid of discrimination

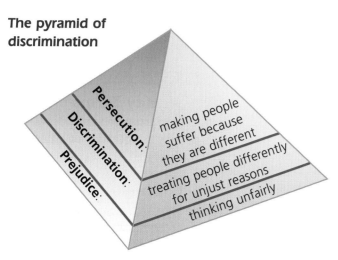

Persecution: making people suffer because they are different

Discrimination: treating people differently for unjust reasons

Prejudice: thinking unfairly

Part of the 'rough and tumble' of schooling?

Lancaster Youth and Community Service set up a group for gay and lesbian young people, to help them cope with the **homophobic** bullying they encountered in schools and colleges. One young man who belongs to the group said, "I love coming here. It's the only time in the week I feel completely safe. It's the one place I can be myself."

1 What does the young man's comment tell you about homophobic bullying?

2 What can schools do to reduce homophobic bullying?

You will find out about discrimination and consider how it affects people and how it might be overcome.

'Education is the answer'

Although there are many black and Asian football players and they are accepted by football fans everywhere, there are still problems with racial prejudice and discrimination. Some fans have been known to call out racist comments and make monkey noises when black players are on the pitch.

Sir Alex Ferguson, Manchester United's manager, is a supporter of football's anti-**racism** campaign, 'Kick It Out!' This is what he says:

"I think it's all down to education and how people are brought up. I was brought up in a family where there was never any prejudice. I think education from family and school is the most important thing. If parents are saying to their kids 'Don't play with that Charlie down the road because he is black,' what message does that give? I think education is the secret."

1 Do you agree with Sir Alex that 'it's all down to education'? Give reasons.
2 Why do you think all top clubs and star football players in the UK support the Kick It Out! campaign?

Young and Powerful

Young and Powerful is a group of young disabled and non-disabled people supported by Comic Relief. They all go to mainstream schools and campaign for **inclusive education**. They believe all children need to be taught together, so they can learn from each other.

1 What does the phrase 'inclusive education' mean?

2 What kinds of physical barriers would a wheelchair-user face if they came to your school? Would they face any other kinds of barriers?

Action

Use the Kick It Out! website, www.kickitout.org, to research what your local football clubs, professional and amateur, are doing to combat racism.

Check your understanding

1 What is prejudice? Why are some people prejudiced against others?
2 What is discrimination? Give some examples.
3 Look at the different cases on these two pages and say whether the people or groups described could have experienced prejudice, discrimination or persecution.
4 How are the people in each story overcoming prejudice?

What's your opinion?

'Discrimination is the result of ignorance.'
Do you agree with this statement? Give reasons for your opinion, showing you have considered another point of view. You might think about fear, ignorance, upbringing, insecurity or bad experiences. Refer to the groups or individuals mentioned on these two pages to support your answers.

Key Terms
homophobic: fearing or hating homosexuals
inclusive education: schooling that involves everyone, regardless of disability or non-disability
racism: the idea that some people of different origins are not as good as others

Discrimination and the law

WHO SAYS ETHNIC MINORITIES CAN'T GET JOBS? THERE ARE OPENINGS EVERYWHERE.

Lavatory attendant. Office cleaner. Somebody has to do all the low-paid, menial jobs, but why is it so often people from ethnic minorities? Prejudice, racial discrimination and harassment are denying people the choice of job they deserve. It's unjust and unfair. More than that, it's a terrible waste of British talent.

COMMISSION FOR RACIAL EQUALITY
CRE Information Section, Elliot House, 10-12 Allington Street, London SW1E 5EH.

1 What message is the poster giving?

2 What other forms of discrimination take place at work?

3 Why do people need protection against discrimination?

4 How do you think the law can help?

Fighting discrimination with the law

Everyone deserves a fair chance to be successful in life. Poster campaigns and other public awareness programmes try to educate people to think beyond prejudice. These campaigns are just one way of dealing with **discrimination**. There are also legal ways of tackling prejudice and discrimination. There are three important anti-discrimination laws:

The Sex Discrimination Act

Sex discrimination generally works against the interests of females, and particularly in the workplace. It can be difficult to ensure that women have the same opportunities for promotion as men, when many have time away at some point to have children. However, although the Act usually protects women, if a man is unfairly treated because he is a man, he is also protected by the Act.

The Race Relations Act

The Race Relations Act makes it an offence to treat a person differently on the grounds of race, colour, nationality, and national or ethnic origin. In practice, most racial discrimination in Britain is against people from ethnic minorities, but people from every nationality are protected by the law.

The Disability Discrimination Act

This Act aims to end discrimination against disabled people. A disability should not stop a person from being employed unless it stops them doing the job. Employers must help their staff. A deaf employee working in an office should be given a videophone to allow them to work like everybody else.

You will discover how the law works to protect people against discrimination.

How has the law helped?

Look at these cases where the anti-discrimination Acts have helped people.

Single mother wins case over 16-hour shifts

A single mother was relieved last night after winning a sex discrimination case. She had been sacked for refusing to work 16-hour shifts at Heathrow airport.

1 Do you think the woman would have won the case if she wasn't a mother and she had refused to work the 16-hour shifts?

2 Do you think a father would have been sacked if he had refused to work 16-hour shifts? What about a single father?

Blind teacher gets £60,000 payout

A blind teacher should have had help from a classroom assistant. She was sacked when the school where she worked decided she had become 'a burden'. An employment tribunal ruled that her school broke the law by failing to provide a classroom assistant to help her.

What explanation might the school give for not wanting to provide a classroom assistant? The court decided this reason was unfair. Explain why.

Ford agrees to stop racism at Dagenham

Ford, the car manufacturing company, apologized and paid **compensation** to four black workers after their faces were replaced by white faces in a sales brochure. Ford then had to pay out more than £70 000 compensation to seven Asian and Afro-Caribbean workers at Dagenham. They were turned down for jobs in the truck fleet, where pay is approximately double the average pay for workers on the shop floor. Less than 2% of workers on the truck fleet are from ethnic minorities, compared with 45% across the factory.

1 Explain why the company had to pay compensation to the four black workers and the seven Asian and Afro-Caribbean workers.

2 What does the figure of 2% of ethnic minorities working in the truck fleet compared with 45% in the rest of the factory suggest about discrimination at the factory at that time?

Action

1 What does your school do to ensure equal opportunities for all students and staff?

2 Contact Scope or look on their website (www.scope.org.uk) and find out about their Schools Access Initiative.

Check your understanding

List the Acts which protect people from discrimination. Think of some situations when people might need to use these laws.

What's your opinion?

'Public awareness campaigns are enough to deal with the problem of discrimination.'
Do you agree with this statement? Give reasons for your opinion, showing you have considered another point of view.

Key Terms

compensation: making amends for something; something given to make good a loss

discrimination (racial, sex and disability): when a person is treated less favourably because of their colour, ethnic origins, gender or disability

What are human rights?

Getting you thinking

1 What are these children deprived of?

2 Make a list of the things you think every child should have.

3 Use your list to write a statement of children's rights.

Human rights

People all over the world suffer because their basic needs are not met. Some people's freedoms are limited by the country in which they live. Nobody should live without these basic **human rights**:

- the right to education
- the right to work
- the right to fair conditions at work
- the right to travel
- the right to food and clothes
- the right to healthcare
- the right to meet with friends
- the right to own property
- the right to follow your religion
- the right to marry and have children
- the rights of minorities to be treated the same as the majority.

1 Which of the rights listed above are the most important to you? Why?

2 Can you think of some situations where any of your rights might be threatened?

3 What examples are there in the news of people's human rights being threatened?

Human rights milestones

Ever since the end of World War II, people have been concerned about human rights. During the war, many people had been badly treated because of their race or religion or because they were prisoners of war.

The case of A versus The United Kingdom

In 1993, a nine-year-old English boy, known as 'A', was beaten with a garden cane by his stepfather. When the stepfather was taken to court, his defence was that English law says a parent can use 'reasonable force' to punish a child. He was found not guilty. The boy's lawyers then took his case to the European Court of Human Rights, which decided the boy had suffered 'cruel, inhuman and degrading punishment'.

The boy was awarded £10 000 in damages and the UK government agreed to change the law to give better protection to children in the future.

You will find out about the development of human rights.

The CRC states: 'Governments should not allow children under 15 to join the army.'

1948
Universal Declaration of Human Rights (UDHR)

The UDHR was drawn up by world leaders who wanted to prevent such terrible things happening again. It states that everyone has a right to life and liberty, freedom of speech and movement, a fair wage, a fair trial, education and many other basic human rights.

1950
The European Convention on Human Rights (ECHR)

This sets the framework for European countries. If the residents of one country don't think they have had a fair response from the courts, they can take their case to the European Court of Human Rights.

1998
Human Rights Act (UK)

Since 2000, the UK has had its own laws on human rights which say that all organizations have a duty to protect the rights of all individuals (as set out in the ECHR). The Human Rights **Act** protects everyone in the UK.

1981
The Convention on the Rights of the Child (CRC)

This **Convention** requires governments all around the world to think about the needs of young people, and to consult them about matters that affect them, such as education, family life, law and order. Millions of young people do not have relatives to look after them; those caught up in civil wars in Africa, for instance. The CRC recognizes this and says that young people must have rights of their own; rights which don't depend on parents or other adults.

Action

Collect newspaper reports and Internet articles concerned with human rights. Discuss the effects that being deprived of these rights can have on people.

Check your understanding

1 Why was the Universal **Declaration** of Human Rights written?
2 What is the main difference between the scope of the Universal Declaration of Human Rights and that of the European Convention on Human Rights?
3 What can European citizens do if they feel their human rights are being denied?
4 Why was the Convention on the Rights of the Child written?

What's your opinion?

'Each country should be able to set its own rules about the rights of its citizens.'
Do you agree with this statement? Give reasons for your opinion, showing you have considered another point of view.

Key Terms

Act: a law passed by Parliament
Convention: an agreement (often between governments)
Declaration: a document setting down aims and intentions
human rights: things that people are morally or legally allowed to do or have

Legal rights

Getting you thinking

1 What do these photographs tell you about human rights in USA in the mid-1900s?

2 Which basic human rights were being denied?

3 Do you think you would see sights like these in the USA today? Give reasons.

What are legal rights?

When law protects a human right, it becomes a **legal right**. For example, everyone has the right to go to public places such as parks, hotels and restaurants. The Race Relations Act makes it illegal for anyone to be refused entry to any public place because of his or her ethnicity. The Act also applies to employment and education.

For example, it is illegal for an employer to tell someone, "You can't have the job because you're black." Similarly, it would be illegal to set up a school that accepted only black students. The Race Relations Act is just one law among many that protects people's rights.

The Universal Declaration of Human Rights says you have a right to a fair wage. The 1998 Minimum Wage Act made this a legal right, so all adult workers in England and Wales must be paid the minimum wage.

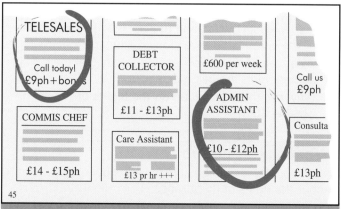

The Universal Declaration of Human Rights also says you have a right to 'equal pay for equal work'. The Sex Discrimination Act made equal pay a legal right.

You will discover how the law is used to protect people's human rights.

Legal rights and age limits

Everyone has basic rights. Some are limited by law.

Some of your legal rights in the UK

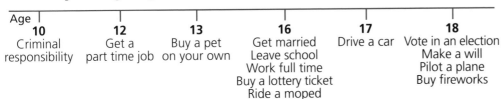

Age					
10	**12**	**13**	**16**	**17**	**18**
Criminal responsibility	Get a part time job	Buy a pet on your own	Get married Leave school Work full time Buy a lottery ticket Ride a moped	Drive a car	Vote in an election Make a will Pilot a plane Buy fireworks

1 Why does the law impose age limits like the ones above?

2 Which of these age limits would you change (raise or lower) and why?

3 Whose human rights are being protected by each of these age limits?

Turning human rights into legal rights

The right to education

The right to work

The right to fair conditions at work

The right to travel

The right to food and clothes

The right to healthcare

The right to meet friends

The right to own property

The right to follow your religion

The right to marry and have children

The rights of minorities to be treated the same as the majority

The right to life

The right to freedom

The right to privacy

The right to fair trial

The right not to be tortured or punished cruelly

The right to vote

1 Can these human rights all be turned into legal rights? Give reasons.

2 Suggest what these laws might say.

Legal rights are looked at throughout this book. You have already seen how there are laws protecting your right to follow your religion, and how the Race Relations Act and The Disability Discrimination Act help to protect the rights of minorities (pages 34–35). In the rest of the course you will learn about laws protecting rights at work (pages 44–45) and laws to do with privacy (pages 94–95).

Action

Research at what age and under what conditions young people have a legal right to drink alcohol. Carry out a survey to find out what your group thinks about these rights and age limits. How easy is it to police these laws?

Check your understanding

1 What is the difference between a human right and a legal right?

2 Name one law which makes a human right a legal right.

3 What does the phrase 'sex discrimination' mean? Give an example.

What's your opinion?

'Legal rights just protect people from themselves.'

Do you agree with this statement? Give reasons for your opinion, showing you have considered another point of view.

Key Terms

legal right: a right which is protected by law

Rights with responsibilities

Getting you thinking

In 2004, over 1100 people were injured by fireworks. Some were seriously hurt.

1 You must be over 18 to buy fireworks, and yet 50 per cent of all injuries were to children under 15. Who do you think is to blame for these accidents?

- companies that make fireworks
- shops which sell fireworks
- parents
- people who organize public displays
- the police
- the children themselves.
  Give reasons.

2 What would you do to reduce the number of accidents with fireworks?

3 Turn your suggestions for question 2 into a firework safety code.

Firework injuries (Oct–Nov 2004) in the UK
Age groups of people injured

Over 20 years 516
Under 13 368
13–17 197
18–20 79

Place where accident occurred

Semi public party (e.g. scouts, club) 63
Large public display 96
Street or other public place 317
Family or private party 590
Other 94

Total injuries 1160

Source: Firework injury statistics, DTI 2004

Rights and responsibilities

Everyone over 18 has a right to buy fireworks. This right, like many others, brings with it certain responsibilities. You must follow the firework code: never throw a lighted firework at anyone, and never set them off in the street where they might disturb elderly neighbours who have a right to peace and quiet, or alarm pets. The age limit for buying fireworks is set by law at 18 because this is the age at which the law expects people to be responsible enough to handle fireworks.

Rights and responsibilities are best thought of as two sides of the same coin. You have a right to own a bike and ride it down your street, but you also have a **responsibility** to ride it carefully so you don't endanger pedestrians or other road users. For example, if you ride without lights in the dark, you could cause a motorist to swerve and crash while trying to avoid you. Even if no one was hurt in the accident, there will be financial consequences for the driver if they need their car to do their job.

You will find out about the link between rights and responsibilities.

All children also have a right to an education, as expressed in the Convention of the Rights of the Child (CRC), but students have a responsibility not to disrupt lessons so others can't learn. You have a right to be respected, but you must also **respect** others. For example, you have a right to follow a particular religion and would expect your religious views to be respected. In the same way, you must respect the religious views of others.

Action

Discuss why people in less economically developed countries (LEDCs) do not have their basic needs.

Check your understanding

1 List some responsibilities that go with the following rights:
   the right to an education; the right to drink alcohol; the right to own and drive a car.
2 Sort the following into two lists: 'Wants' and 'Needs'.
   Healthy food; 'A' levels; holidays; fashionable clothes; a good job; friends; healthcare; pocket money; TV in your room; clean air; free travel to school; sex education; parents/adults who look after you.
3 Now add five or six more items to each list.

What's your opinion?

'People should never have rights without responsibilities.'
Do you agree with this statement? Give reasons for your opinion, showing you have considered another point of view.

Needs and wants

What you have a right to and what you want are not the same thing. For instance, the Convention on the Rights of the Child states that you have the right to 'clean water and healthy food'. You might say, "I don't like drinking water. I want cola or coffee!" But the CRC focuses on the most basic human rights and needs, which are denied to millions of people all over the world: it isn't about 'wants'.

As living standards rise and countries become richer, people's 'wants' increase too. Most UK families would say that televisions, washing machines, central heating and fridges are 'basic' household items, but our great-grandparents would have considered them luxuries.

Key Terms

respect: to have a good opinion of someone
responsibility: something it is your duty to do or to look after

Protecting the customer

They said it would remove oil and grease but it doesn't. I followed the washing instructions, but the colours ran and stained all my other clothes.

These shoes just don't suit me. They looked good when I tried them on in the shop.

I bought a computer over the Internet, but it doesn't work. The company I bought it from says I have signed my rights away.

1 Match these questions to the situations. Can I get my money back? Can I get compensation? Can that be true?

2 Who do you think is at fault in each of the examples: the retailer, manufacturer or consumer?

3 Are there any examples where the consumer is to blame?

What are my rights?

When you buy something from a shop, by mail order or over the Internet, you are called a **consumer** and, as a consumer, you have certain rights. You are also a consumer when you pay someone to provide a service, such as a hairdresser, a photographer or an accountant.

Some of the most important laws protecting consumers' rights include:

- the *Trade Descriptions Act*, which makes it a criminal offence to make misleading price claims about goods or services. For example, "Was £200. Now £149.99" is misleading if the goods have never been sold at the higher price. If a film processor offers a one-hour service, this must be true.

- the *Sale and Supply of Goods Act*, which is concerned that goods sold must be of satisfactory quality and fit for the purpose they are sold and advertised for.

- the *Food Safety Act*, which covers the preparation and selling of food and drink in both shops and restaurants. The Act makes it an offence to sell or serve food or drink that is unsafe.

- the *Consumer Protection Act*, which means that consumers can claim for damages if they are injured as a result of using faulty goods. If a child was hurt by an unsafe toy, the manufacturers could be prosecuted.

Food safety officers have the power to inspect food that is being processed or that is for sale. Restaurants can be closed down if they serve unsafe food or drink

You will find out about laws which help consumers get a fair deal.

How can you enforce your rights?

If you have bought goods or services and you are dissatisfied with them, you have a right to claim your money back, to an exchange or to a repeat of the service.

1 Contact the trader with details of your complaint, say what you want done and give them a chance to put the matter right.

2 If you are not happy with the outcome, you can seek advice from the **Citizens Advice Bureau (CAB)**. They can help with a wide variety of problems, including shopping complaints.

3 The Citizens Advice Bureau may recommend you go to a **Trading Standards Department**. They can investigate complaints about misleading descriptions or prices, and the safety of consumer goods. They can take action against people who break the law.

4 The **Office of Fair Trading**, a government office, can also take action against traders who break consumer laws.

Action

Working in pairs, think about why traders and businesses prefer to sort out complaints themselves.

Check your understanding

1 If you bought a CD at a reduced price because the CD cover was damaged, would you be able to take it back to the shop and claim a refund? Give reasons for your answer.
2 If you bought something from a shop and it was faulty, but the shop refused to refund your money, what could you do?
3 What extra rights do you have when home shopping or shopping over the Internet, compared with when you buy something from a shop?

What's your opinion?

'Consumers should look after themselves.'
Do you agree with this statement? Give reasons for your opinion, showing you have considered another point of view.

Sellers have rights too

Consumers cannot claim refunds or demand exchanges in certain situations. If you bought a shirt in a sale and you knew it had a defect, you would not be able to claim your money back, because the seller didn't hide the problem from you when you bought it.

Sellers do not have to exchange goods, but most will do so as long as they have not been used. So, if you have bought some clothes and you change your mind about them later, you will find most shops are happy to exchange them, even though they don't have to by law.

Home shopping and the Internet

When you buy over the Internet from a company trading in the UK, you are covered by more or less the same legislation as those that cover shop purchases:

- the goods you've bought should be of satisfactory quality
- they should be fit for the purpose they are sold for
- they should be as described by the seller.

Key Terms

Citizens Advice Bureau (CAB): an organization that offers free advice on consumer and other legal matters

consumer: a person who buys goods or services for their own needs

Office of Fair Trading: a government office that can take action against traders who break the law

Trading Standards Department: an official body that enforces consumer-based laws

Fair play at work

Getting you thinking

Many people work on computers all day. Their employers may have set them tough targets to meet.

1 What sorts of problems do you think people might face when at work?

2 How do you think an employer might make their staff's working life better?

3 What effect do you think a happy workforce has on a business?

4 What do you think the law should have to say about working conditions?

Why do we need employment laws?

Employment laws exist to protect employees and make sure businesses carry out their responsibilities towards their staff. Without these laws, people's human right to fair conditions at work could be harder to protect.

Exploiting people

Before laws were introduced to protect people, some employers treated their staff unfairly. Employees suffered though:

• long hours

• dangerous and unhealthy working conditions

• poor pay

• not being treated as individuals, with individual needs.

There was no government support in terms of unemployment benefit or sickness pay, so employees could not afford to argue with their employers, nor could they afford to be ill.

Unions

Employees began to form **trade unions**. They negotiated with employers to reach fairer agreements on pay and working conditions. Over the years, these agreements have led to huge improvements in the rights of employees.

By trying to persuade employers and Parliament to adopt fairer and safer working practices, the unions proved to be effective **pressure groups** in looking after the interests of their members. A group of people bargaining together is more powerful than individuals working alone.

Unions helped to form the Labour Party

How does the law protect?

The Equal Pay Act means that men and women in jobs which require the same effort, skills or responsibility should be paid the same amount.

The Contract of Employment is an agreement between employer and employee setting out the pay and conditions, including holiday entitlements.

The Sex Discrimination Act and the Race Relations Act protect individuals from being treated differently because of their sex, nationality or ethnicity.

Health and safety laws are designed to reduce accidents. Employers must provide a safe working environment and train employees to work safely.

European regulations

Some **European Union** members have signed up to a Social Chapter. The Chapter sets employment rights, such as maternity and paternity leave, so that everyone has guaranteed working conditions.

The UK has not signed the Chapter because higher wages and better conditions would push up the business costs. UK businesses would therefore become less competitive as prices would rise and it would be harder to sell their products. This might mean that the number of jobs in the UK fell.

Action
1 Find out what unions provide for their members.
2 Produce a union recruitment poster giving reasons why employees should join. You can get ideas from www.tuc.org.uk or www.unison.org.uk.

Check your understanding
1 Who do unions represent and what are they trying to do?
2 What areas do the main employment laws cover?

What's your opinion?
'The UK should sign the EU's Social Chapter.'
Do you agree with this statement? Give reasons for your opinion, showing you have considered another point of view

Key Terms
employment laws: laws passed by Parliament and by the European Union law-making bodies that set out the rights and responsibilities of employers and employees

European Union: a group of 25 countries that works together in fields such as the environment, social issues, the economy and trade

pressure group: a group of people that tries to change public opinion or government policy to its own views or beliefs

trade unions: organizations that look after the interests of a group of employees

Responsibilities in the workplace

Getting you thinking

1 Explain each of ASDA's rules.

2 Why does ASDA expect its staff to have a responsible attitude to their work?

3 ASDA expects its staff to be responsible. What should the staff expect from ASDA?

What Asda expects from you

Attendance

If you don't come to work, your work has to be done by your colleagues and it reduces our opportunity to offer good customer service. However, sometimes absence from work is unavoidable. If you can't come to work, please contact the store no later than two hours before the start of your shift.

Punctuality

Customers expect us to be available to give them the service they want, so all colleagues must avoid lateness.

Appearance

Colleagues must wear the uniform provided by the Company and adhere to the dress standards.

Friends and relatives

Colleagues must not serve relatives or friends at either counters or checkouts.

Mobile phones

Colleagues are allowed to make personal calls during their break times from pay phones provided in store. Colleagues may not carry or use personal mobile phones whilst working.

Your responsibilities as an employee

Just as employers have responsibilities towards their employees, so the employees have responsibilities towards their employer.

Employees must carry out their responsibilities as set out in the **contract of employment**. Employees should receive this within eight weeks of starting a new job. This contract sets out what the employer and the employee are expected to do. This is important: there are two sides to the contract and both the employer and employee must do what they have agreed to. If the employee fails to do this, they can be dismissed. If the employer doesn't keep their side of the contract, the employee can take them to an **employment tribunal**.

A contract should include the following:
- names of employer and employee
- entitlement to sick pay
- date of starting
- pension details (if any)
- rate of pay and working hours
- complaints and disciplinary procedures
- place of work
- conditions for ending the employment contract
- holiday entitlement.

You will understand that both employers and employees have responsibilities in the workplace.

What if it goes wrong?

People can be dismissed if they are unable to do the job properly or have been involved in any misconduct, such as fighting, discrimination, deliberate damage or theft. A minor misconduct, such as bad timekeeping, usually results in a verbal **warning**. If this continues, it will become a written warning and, with no further improvement, can end in **dismissal**. A major misconduct, like theft, can lead to instant dismissal.

Dismissal is different from **redundancy**. Redundancy occurs when the job has ended and no one is being taken on to replace you. It is the employer's responsibility and the employee will receive a payment at least equivalent to one month's pay for every year employed by the business.

Disagreements over dismissal

There might be a disagreement between the employer and the employee over a dismissal. If it can't be sorted out, the case can be taken to an employment tribunal. This is a type of court of law that has the power to fine the business and make it pay damages to the employee if it finds that the employee was not to blame. If the dismissed person belongs to a union, they can seek advice from it and the union can represent them at the tribunal. Sometimes tribunals come out in favour of the employer and sometimes in favour of the employee.

Action

Look in a local or national paper to see if there are any reports of an industrial tribunal. What was the issue? Who won? Why? Had one side acted irresponsibly? If so, explain how.

Check your understanding

1 What is the contract of employment for?
2 What reasons can be given for dismissal?
3 What is the difference between dismissal and redundancy?
4 What can an employee do if they feel they have been treated unfairly?

What's your opinion?

'Rights at work are more important than responsibilities.'
Do you agree with this statement? Give reasons for your opinion, showing you have considered another point of view.

Key Terms

contract of employment: a document that details an employee's and employer's responsibilities for a particular job

dismissal: when employers end an employee's contract of employment (sometimes called 'sacking')

employment tribunal: a type of court dealing only with disagreements over employment laws

redundancy: when a person loses their job because the job doesn't need to be done anymore

warning: written or spoken warning given by an employer to an employee if the employer thinks the employee has been breaking the contract of employment

What's the point of law?

Getting you thinking

This group of friends all live together. They left home a year ago and rent a house together. Two of them work during the day, one sometimes works a night shift and two are students.

1 What kinds of things do they have to think about and remember to do because they live together? Might there be any situations that could lead to disagreements between them?

2 Imagine you are in a similar situation. Which rules would you make to ensure that the house ran as smoothly as possible?

Why do people obey the law?

Law-abiding citizens obey the law for a variety of reasons: they may have strong religious or moral views about breaking the law; they may be afraid of being caught and arrested; they may fear the shame that going to prison would bring on them and their family; they may be worried about damaging their 'good name' (their reputation).

In some situations it is obvious why a law is needed. If drivers drove through traffic lights on 'stop', they could be seriously injured or killed, or cause injury or death to someone else.

Why do we need laws?

The short answer is, try imagining life without them! Your life would be chaotic, and the most vulnerable members of society, such as the very young, the elderly, the ill and some minorities, would suffer most. What would happen to children, for example, if there were no laws on divorce?

For laws to work properly they need the support of the majority of the population. Most people agree that child abuse is a shocking crime and abusers must be punished.

But public opinion is more divided on euthanasia. Some think it wrong to treat doctors as criminals if they help terminally ill patients in pain to die. Others would argue that this is morally wrong as well as unlawful.

You will understand why we need laws.

Who's the loser?

A shoplifter, who has stolen a couple of T-shirts, might argue that their actions won't put a big company like Marks and Spencer out of business. But:

* if everybody stole from them it would push up prices for everyone else who shops there, because Marks and Spencer had to pay for the T-shirts

* if you steal from Marks and Spencer, you steal from the people who own the business, so it's just like stealing a mobile phone or a car.

In the same way, if people don't pay income tax when they should, the government will have less money to pay for schools and hospitals; so many people are affected indirectly by tax evasion.

Action

1 In groups, think about your usual daily routine and list how many times during the day you come across a rule or law. Why do you choose to obey or not to obey these rules and laws?

2 You sometimes hear people say "But it's a bad law." Make a list of your reasons for laws being good or bad. Be ready to explain your ideas.

Check your understanding

1 In your own words, give four reasons why people obey the law. Suggest one more reason not mentioned on these pages.

2 Make a list of crimes that have immediate consequences for the general public. List others that may have long-term and less immediate consequences.

3 Why do you think it is important that the majority of citizens support a particular law? Suggest one law that probably has majority support. Suggest one that probably doesn't, and give a reason.

What's your opinion?

'You should never break the law.'
Do you agree with this statement? Give reasons for your opinion, showing you have considered another point of view.

Why do laws change?

There are laws to cover a vast range of activities, including adoption, marriage and divorce, terrorism, discrimination, motoring, banking, sex, drugs, theft and assault. New developments, such as cloning or the Internet, often require new laws.

1.3: Criminal and civil justice

Civil and criminal law: what's the difference?

Getting you thinking

Neighbours go to court over right to access land

Police raid drug den

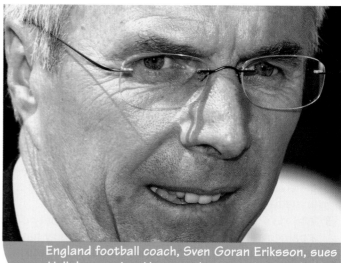

1 Which case is a private issue?

2 Which case is more likely to have the police involved? Give reasons.

3 Which case is more worrying for the general public? Why?

Two kinds of law

Over many centuries of law making, two separate but related branches of the law have evolved to meet changing circumstances: **civil law** and **criminal law**.

Most civil cases are about disputes between individuals or groups, and very often these arguments are about rights. Examples include company law, adoption, accidents at work and consumer rights.

Criminal law deals with offences such as murder, theft and drug dealing. In a criminal case, the conflict is between the government (acting for all citizens) and the lawbreakers.

Who's right?

The person who brings a case to a civil court is called the claimant. The person accused of doing wrong is called the defendant. In some civil cases, the claimant sets out to **sue** the defendant. If the claimant wins, the defendant will have to give them money.

England football coach, Sven Goran Eriksson, sues Hello! magazine. He says the magazine invaded his privacy and published photographs of his home without his permission.

1 Who is the claimant in the Sven-Goran Eriksson case? Who is the defendant?

2 Why will this case be heard in a civil court?

You will find out about the difference between civil and criminal law.

A civil court
A **judge** sitting without a **jury** decides almost all civil cases.

Criminal courts
There is a separate system of courts to deal with criminal cases. Less serious offences are dealt with in **magistrates' courts**. Serious offences are dealt with in **crown courts** before a judge and a jury.

Action
Make a list of the different kind of cases that appear in civil courts. Which human rights are involved in each type?

Check your understanding
1 What are the main differences between civil and criminal cases?
2 What is (a) a claimant, (b) a defendant and (c) a small claims court?
3 What type of crime is dealt with in either the magistrates' or crown courts?

What's your opinion?
'Neighbours should sort things out instead of going to court.'
Do you agree with this statement? Give reasons for your opinion, showing you have considered another point of view.

What happens in a civil court?
Most civil cases are heard in a **county court**. Because a court case can be very expensive, most people try to settle the dispute before it gets to court.

A small number of civil cases are heard in a **High Court**. These courts deal with complex family disputes and other complicated financial and legal matters, such as bankruptcy and large claims for damages. Any case involving £50 000 or more is heard in the High Court.

If a civil case involves a claim of less than £5000, it will be heard in a **small claims court**. About 90 000 cases a year are heard in these courts.

Key Terms
civil law: this covers disputes between individuals or groups. Civil law cases are often about rights between people

county court: a local court that has limited powers in civil cases

criminal law: this deals with offences such as murder and drug dealing. These cases are between the Crown Prosecution Service (acting for all citizens) and the offender

crown court: courts held in towns in England and Wales where judges hear cases

High Court: the court where judges hear cases on serious crimes

judge: a person who decides questions of law in a court

jury: a group of people who decide if someone is guilty in a court of law

magistrates' court: a court held before two or more public officers dealing with minor crimes

small claims court: a local court, which hears civil cases involving small amounts of money

sue: to make a claim against someone or something

1.3: Criminal and civil justice

Who puts the law into practice?

Getting you thinking

1 You've broken the law and have to appear in court. Which of the following would you prefer as your 'judge and jury', and why?

- your teachers
- your classmates
- your parents
- the police
- other young people who've been in trouble themselves
- the victims of your crime
- a group of people chosen at random, who do not know you.

2 Which group do you think the victim would prefer? Give reasons.

3 Which group do you think would give the fairest outcome? Give reasons.

The criminal justice system

The criminal justice system is large and complex. These are the roles within it.

Judges

The judges who work in both criminal and civil courts are known collectively as the **judiciary**. Most judges have worked for at least ten years as a barrister, but a few solicitors also become judges. In a jury trial, it is the jury who decide if the accused is guilty or not, but the judge who determines the sentence.

Senior judges (who sit in the higher courts) are very powerful. They don't make laws: Parliament does that. But if there is an argument about how a law should be interpreted, it is the senior judges who decide.

Magistrates

Full-time magistrates

Full-time (paid) magistrates are called district judges. They are usually barristers or solicitors with at least seven years' experience. They sit alone.

Part-time magistrates

Part-time magistrates come from all walks of life. They are not legally qualified and are not paid. They work with other magistrates.

Jury

A jury is made up of 12 adults, who sit in a crown court and decide whether the accused person is innocent or guilty. A jury is made up of members of the public chosen at random.

You will find out about the various roles of people who work within the criminal justice system.

Police
The police do not make laws: they enforce them. Their job is to protect the public, arrest lawbreakers and bring them before the courts.

Solicitors
All **solicitors** must pass law exams because, among other things, they can give legal advice to people who have to go to court. Some solicitors also speak in court on behalf of their clients.

Barristers
Barristers undergo a long legal training too, but they spend most of their time in court representing their clients. They are the only lawyers qualified to speak in any type of court.

Probation officers
If an offender is given a community sentence (see page 56–57), they will work with a local **probation officer**. Probation officers are professionally qualified. They write court reports on offenders and supervise them in the community when they've been sentenced.

Action
1 Research the entry requirements (that is, age, qualifications, etc.) of either a police officer or a solicitor.
2 Interview a probation officer to find out about the work they do with offenders in the community. You may wish to research a specific aspect of their work. For example, probation officers often work with young offenders who have problems with alcohol and other drugs.
3 Research who can be called for jury service and what serving on a jury involves.

Check your understanding
1 What do judges do in trials where there is a jury?
2 What powers do senior judges have?
3 What is the most important difference between the role of the police and the role of judges?
3 What is the difference between a barrister and a solicitor?
4 What skills and personal qualities do you think you need to be a good magistrate?
5 Can you think of any reasons why people don't apply to be magistrates?

Key Terms
barrister: a lawyer who represents and speaks for their clients in court
judiciary: all the judges in a country
probation officer: someone who writes court reports on offenders and supervises them in the community
solicitor: a lawyer who gives legal advice and may speak for their clients in court

Criminal courts

1 Which of the two courtrooms above is the most 'child-friendly' and why?

2 Should courts be made more 'adult-friendly'? Give reasons.

3 Is it good idea that courts are open to the public? Give reasons.

Two types of court

Courts are formal places. Everyone involved must take the process very seriously. In some countries, youth courts are more informal because people think young people are more likely to tell the truth in a more relaxed environment.

There are two types of court for criminal cases: magistrates' courts and crown courts.

A magistrates' court

Over 95 per cent of all criminal trials take place in magistrates' courts. Specially-trained magistrates also run youth courts for offenders aged between 10 and 17. Magistrates, who sit in court with at least one other magistrate, also deal with a small number of civil cases.

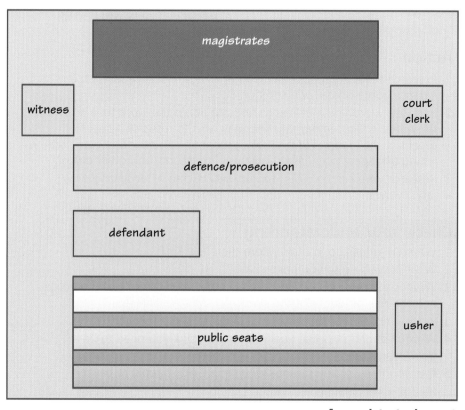

A magistrates' court

You will find out about the differences between a magistrates' court and a crown court.

Mitigating factors

There is no jury in a magistrates' court, so magistrates must be absolutely sure 'beyond reasonable doubt' that the accused is guilty. They must also take into account any **mitigating** factors. If, for example, a woman stole from a supermarket because she had no money to buy food for herself and her children, magistrates would take this into account and might give her a lesser sentence.

What sentences can magistrates give?

Magistrates have the power to give the following penalties:

- prison: up to a maximum of six months
- community sentences*
- Antisocial Behaviour Orders or ASBOs
- fines: of up to a maximum £5000
- discharge: conditional or absolute*
  (*see page 57)

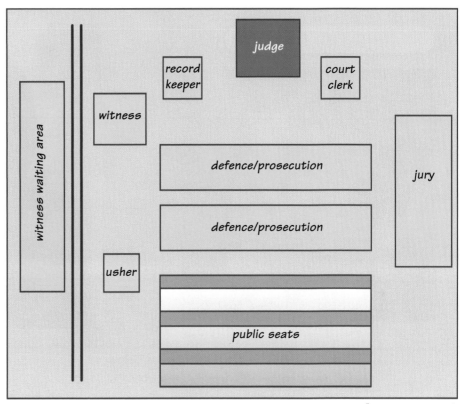

A crown court

A crown court

The most serious criminal cases are heard in a crown court. The atmosphere is more solemn and the proceedings are more formal than in a magistrates' court. The judges and barristers wear wigs and gowns. A jury decides if the defendant is guilty or not (unless the defendant pleads guilty, in which case no jury is involved).

Crown court judges can have different powers. Only High Court judges, who sit in the larger courts, can try very serious cases, such as murder and rape. Others, known as circuit judges and **recorders**, try less serious cases such as theft, for example.

Crown court judges and juries must also take into account any mitigating factors, in the same way that magistrates do. The maximum sentence in a crown court is life imprisonment.

Check your understanding

1 What are 'mitigating factors'? Support your answer with an example.
2 What kinds of mitigating factors might influence magistrates' decisions when sentencing young offenders?
3 List the differences between a magistrates' court and crown court.
4 What is the maximum sentence each type of court can impose?
5 When is a jury used in a crown court case?

What's your opinion?

'Courts should be friendlier places.'
Do you agree with this statement? Give reasons for your opinion, showing you have considered another point of view.

Key Terms

mitigating: making something less intense or severe

recorder: a barrister or solicitor of at least ten years' experience, who acts as a part-time judge in a crown court

What sentence?

Getting you thinking

Mrs B stole £500

Mr G stole £50

Look at the list of possible decisions below. Which would be the fairest? Give reasons.

- Both Mrs B and Mr G should get the same sentence.

- Mrs B should get a tougher sentence because she stole more.

- Mrs B should get a lighter sentence because she is old and poor.

- Mrs B should get a lighter sentence because she's a woman.

Making the punishment fit the crime

There is a range of sentences available to magistrates and judges. Sentences must follow guidelines laid down by the government, but these do allow some flexibility. It would be undesirable to have only one sentence for theft, for instance, as this might result in someone who stole £10 receiving the same punishment as someone who stole £10 000.

What's the point of punishment?

Which of the five reasons on the right for punishing offenders do you think is the most important, and why? Which is the least important?

Punishment	Separation from friends and family, and the 'outside world'.
Public protection	Did victims and others feel safer when they were locked up?
Deterrence	Will the punishment stop them re-offending? Will it stop others offending?
Rehabilitation	Have they learned any useful skills while they were inside? Have they learned to cope with their anger? Their drugs problem?
Disapproval	Do they feel ashamed? Do they understand how law-abiding people feel about their crime?

You will discover how magistrates and judges fit the sentence to the crime.

Prison

You will be sent to prison if you commit a serious crime (for example, armed robbery), but only if you are over 21. Young offenders (18–21) are sent to a Young Offenders Institution.

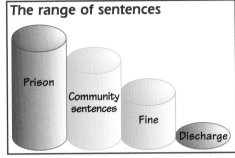

The range of sentences

Prison

Community sentences

Fine

Discharge

Community sentences

If you are given a **community sentence**, you don't go to prison. You will work with a probation officer in the community. If a community service order is imposed, you will work a set number of hours (usually at the weekend) cleaning up graffiti and litter, tidying gardens or building playgrounds.

If a curfew order is also imposed, you must be at home for up to 12 hours each day and electronic tags may be used to check on your whereabouts. If you have a problem with alcohol or other drugs, you may have to undergo regular drug tests and attend drug treatment classes.

An exclusion order prohibits you from going to pubs, football grounds and other places where you've previously caused trouble. Persistent offenders might receive an Antisocial Behaviour Order (ASBO), which restricts the movements of persistent offenders.

A reparation order means you do work for your victims (if they agree) to make up for any harm you did, financial or emotional.

Fines

Crown courts can impose unlimited fines, but the maximum fine in a magistrates' court is £5000. Any fine must reflect the offender's ability to pay. The maximum fine for 14- to 17-year-olds is £1000.

Discharge

If you are a first-time offender who has committed a minor offence, having to go to court is seen as punishment enough and you will probably get an absolute discharge. If you are given a conditional discharge, you will have to keep out of trouble for a set period or you will be punished for the original offence.

Appeals

If you are found guilty but you do not think you had a fair trial, or you think the sentence is too harsh, you can, in certain circumstances, **appeal** against the sentence.

If you were found guilty in a magistrates' court, your appeal would usually be heard in a crown court.

Everyone has the right to appeal, but an appeal will only go ahead if you have a good reason. For instance, if your case had a lot of press coverage, this may have influenced the jury. If someone is convicted and their sentence seems light, the prosecutor can appeal too.

Rapper, Michael Junior Harvey of So Solid Crew, was sentenced to 150 hours of community service for assaulting a police officer.

Action

Research ways in which community service orders are used with young offenders in your area. Are they 'a soft option'?

Check your understanding

1 When might a magistrate impose an exclusion order?
2 What is the difference between an absolute discharge and a conditional discharge?
3 What are the two main reasons for appealing against a sentence?

What's your opinion?

'An offender's punishment continues after their sentence has been served.'
Do you agree with this statement? Give reasons for your opinion, showing you have considered another point of view.

Key Terms

appeal: a request for a decision made by a court to be reviewed

community sentence: when someone who has been convicted of a crime works in the community (clearing litter, for example) rather than going to prison

rehabilitation: restoring a person to normal life

Human rights: the exam

Evidence-based questions

Right to work: rights at work

   Tom, Mary and Asif all went to the same school. Asif is of Asian descent and Tom and Mary are white. They all left school at 16 with broadly similar qualifications.

   Two years later they have the same job titles and work the same hours. Mary is paid £5.00 an hour. Tom gets £6.00 an hour and Asif only receives £3.00 an hour. He has a speech disability but his manager admits that his work is as good as that of other workers.

   They receive a leaflet from a trade union. From this they find out about contracts of employment; discipline codes, involving final warnings prior to dismissal; and laws such as the Sex Discrimination Act, the Race Relations Act, the Minimum Wage Act and the Disability Discrimination Act.

   The three are surprised to discover that their pay rates are different when they chat about the leaflet. Mary and Asif complain to their managers. Although they have never been accused of any misconduct, both are immediately dismissed.

1. Suggest two ways in which Mary's legal rights have been broken.   *(2 marks)*

   1. Mary is paid less than Tom for doing the same work, so the Equal Pay Act has been broken.

   2. The Sex Discrimination Act says she should be treated the same as a male in the same job.

2. Suggest two other ways in which Asif's legal rights may have been broken.   *(2 marks)*

   1. Asif has been discriminated against because of his ethnic origins, so the Race Relations Act has been broken.

   2. Asif is paid less than the others, although he does the same job despite his speech problems.

   > You might also have said that as he only gets £3.00 an hour, he is paid below the minimum wage. The law was also broken because both Mary and Asif were sacked without going through the proper procedures.

3. Outline three steps businesses should take when dealing with employee misconduct   *(3 marks)*
   before reaching the stage of dismissal.

   1. Verbal warning

   2. Written warning

   3. Final warning

Here are some real exam questions on the theme of Human rights. They are taken from sections B and C of the exam. Read the questions, answers and comments from an examiner carefully and think about how you would answer them.

4. Study the evidence and use your own knowledge. *(2 marks)*

Suggest two practical steps that Mary or Asif could take in order to get their dismissal reversed.

1. Talk to the trade union, because their contracts of employment have probably been broken.
2. They could appeal against their dismissal either to their employees or at an employment tribunal.

Leave margin blank

> Remember that you need to bring in some of your own ideas here. The answer doesn't just come from the passage.

Source: Edexcel Citizenship Studies 2004

Short answer questions

1. At what age does a young person first gain the rights and responsibilities listed below? *(4 marks)*

Age	10	12	16	17
Becoming criminally responsible	✓	☐	☐	☐
Can drive a car	☐	☐	☐	✓
Can get a part-time job	☐	✓	☐	☐
Can get married	☐	☐	✓	☐

> There are all sorts of communities. Supporters of Manchester United, Norwich City or Brentford all form communities. People's religion often makes them a member of a community. Members of a choir or charity organization would also count as communities. Just choose an example you know about.

2. Give and define one example of a community. *(2 marks)*

A community is a group of people who are interested in the same things or have the same values. People who live in a village or one area of a town often form a community.

3. Why is it often suggested that most people belong to more than one community? *(1 mark)*

People might belong to a community where they live as well as belonging to a club or religious group.

4. Identify any 2 human rights enjoyed by UK citizens. *(2 marks)*

   1. *Right to be free from discrimination.*
   2. *Right to education*

> There are many more which you can draw from the Declaration of Human Rights. These include the right to life, health or being treated equally under the law.

5. What action can be taken by UK citizens who believe they have been denied their human rights? *(1 mark)*

   You can go to the British courts if you have been discriminated against.

> If human rights have been infringed and there is no way of getting redress in Britain, you can go the European Court of Human Rights.

6. What is a jury? *(1 mark)*

   A jury is a group of people, chosen at random from the population, who decide whether someone is innocent or guilty in a criminal court.

7. The new digital camera you purchased on Monday fails to work properly on the following Wednesday. The shop says it will give you a replacement or a credit note or send the camera to the manufacturer but you decide you want your money back. What are you rights? *(1 mark)*

   You have the right to get your money back.

> The answer to this question is very short, but right! Don't waste time writing more than you need.

Source: Edexcel Citizenship Studies 2003, 2004, 2005

Extended writing

'Breaking the law is never justified.'

Do you agree with this view?

Give reasons for your opinion, showing you have considered another point of view.

You could include some of the following points in your answer and other information of your own. You should support your points with examples, wherever possible.

- Is the law always right and should people who disagree with the law break it?
- Are stealing or speeding justifiable in an emergency?
- If we all have the right to live in a law-abiding society, don't we all have a duty to obey the laws?
- If we dislike a law, shouldn't we campaign against it peacefully and avoid causing damage or injury?
- Is there a difference between the law and moral codes? *(9 marks)*

Source: Edexcel Citizenship Studies 2005

I don't think the law is always right but people should try not to break it. Sometimes it is hard not to. If someone is seriously ill and you are taking them to hospital, you might want to go faster than the speed limit. You are breaking the law but might save someone's life. Stealing is more difficult. If someone is hungry, there are people who can help. Shoplifting doesn't seem to hurt anyone but every time something is stolen, it pushes up the price for everyone else.

> The answer shows that the student is looking at the bullet points and thinking about each one, not just copying them down.

We can't just pick and choose which laws we keep unless there is a special reason. We all want to live in a safe society and therefore we must keep the law. In some places, people behave very badly and make it hard for people to live their everyday lives. There are some places where there are lots of young people with ASBOs because they won't keep the law.

> This shows that the student is using information they have learnt during the course to support their argument.

Lots of people dislike different laws. If people hadn't protested strongly women might still not have the vote. Sometimes it seems necessary to break the law to get noticed. Peaceful protest is not enough. When the government passes laws that people dislike, there are often protests. When fox hunting was banned, people invaded the House of Commons, and were fined for doing so.

> The answer shows another point of view. If it didn't, it could only get half marks.

People who have strong religious beliefs often have different moral codes. Some religions don't believe in abortion, for example, but the law allows them. They often want to ban it. I don't think that people who hold different moral beliefs should be able to interfere with how other people behave, as long as it's within the law of the country.

> Again, there are two points of view. The student explains his or her own views.

I think that we should try to keep the law as much as possible. Sometimes it may be necessary to break it because the law isn't right or it might mean saving a life.

> Each paragraph shows how the student has weighed up each bullet point and explained the point of view. At the end, there is a conclusion which shows they have considered different points of view.

Theme 2 Power, politics

and the media

Taking part

Getting you thinking

School council

The school council will meet at 3.30 p.m. on 1 February in room SL13. Please make sure that all year groups have discussed the issues on the agenda with their representatives so that decisions can be taken at the meeting. If there are other issues you want to raise, please discuss them in form time before the meeting.

Y10 community service teams

Briefing will take place at 1.20 p.m. next Tuesday. Please be sure to have told Mr Jones which task team you want to be in.

Concert rehearsals

The dress rehearsal for the concert is taking place on Thursday. Please turn up on time for your item. There are over 100 people involved, so timing is important.

Ski trip

Anyone in Years 9, 10 or 11 who is interested in joining the ski trip to Italy next year, please come to a meeting at 1.20 p.m. in room SR6 on Wednesday 7 February.

School football team comes top of the league again!

Congratulations to all those who have taken part. The season is not yet over but no one can overtake us now. The last three games might make it a year to remember!

New headteacher

Interviews for the new headteacher take place next week. They will be viewing the school on Tuesday morning. The student interview panel should please report to the school office at 2 p.m. on Tuesday afternoon.

1 Make a list of the different ways in which students can take part in the life of this school.

2 How many other ways can you participate at your school?

3 Do you think it is important to have a wide range of ways that students can participate? Give reasons.

4 Do you think taking part in school activities affects how students think about the school?

Joining in

All schools have different ways in which students can join in. For example, there are stories of students painting the social areas of their school or making an environmental garden, and many schools run projects where students work together to combat problems such as bullying.

All these ways of joining in help people to have more respect for the school and their fellow students. If you have created and looked after something, or have worked hard to make the school a better place, you want it to stay like that. If you see others spoiling it in some way, you will probably want to stop them.

A school where there is lots of participation is likely to have many students who have a sense of belonging and, therefore, respect its way of life.

Students and staff during a school council meeting

You will investigate how and why people participate in the life of the school in order to understand how democracy works.

Having a voice

There are other activities that help to run the school. Do you have a school council? In most cases where they operate, every class and year group has a representative on the **school council**. Sometimes there may be year-group councils, because younger students can find it hard to be heard when in meetings with older students. The school council will discuss things that they want changing, or comment on proposals from the staff.

When all students in school feel that they have a voice, they are likely to be happier about the decisions that are made.

Choosing the representatives

When classes have to choose a member of the school council, they usually do it by holding an **election**. Students can volunteer to stand, or they might be put forward by their friends. They are often asked to make a speech about their views, after which an election is held. In the election, everyone in the class can vote for the person who they want to be the class representative. The one with the most votes will join the school council. This representative will be responsible for listening to their classmates' opinions and standing up for these views in school council meetings. There are too many students in every school for every individual opinion to be heard, so having one person to represent a group is a practical system.

This process of choosing and electing representatives is known as **representative democracy**, a system in which people have a chance to vote for someone who they want to represent them. This happens in schools all over the country, but it also happens in elections in your local area and the whole country.

The level of involvement of the council can vary, but many are consulted when important decisions, such as teacher appointments, are made. One newly appointed deputy headteacher said, "The toughest part of the whole interview was the one with the students." It was tough because he respected the students' views and knew that these were the people he had to be able to influence if he was to have a successful future. It's much easier to work with people if they respect you.

Choosing a representative in a national election

Action

Does your school have a school council? If it does, what has it discussed recently? If it doesn't have a council, do you think it should? Why?

Check your understanding

1 In your own words, say why it can be useful to have a school council.
2 What does 'representative democracy' mean?

What's your opinion?

'It's easier to work with people if they respect you.'
Do you agree with this statement? Give reasons for your opinion, showing you have considered another point of view. Think of examples where working together could be made easier if those taking part had more respect for each other.

Key Terms

election: selection of one or more people for an official position by voting

representative democracy: a type of democracy where citizens have the right to choose someone to represent them on a council or in Parliament as an MP

school council: a group of people who represent the classes and year groups of the school. They give students the opportunity to participate in decision making

Who represents us?

Getting you thinking

Don't close the skate park!

Joe had arranged to meet his friends down at the local skate park. When he arrived, no one was skating. Everyone was talking in one corner, all sounding very angry. They were looking at a notice pinned to the wall that read: THE SKATE PARK WILL CLOSE ON 31 OCTOBER.

No one had been told about the closure and everyone was asking questions: "Why?"; "Who decided?"; "What about us?"; "What can we do about it?"

Joe suggested that they could complain to the local **council**. The council had become involved when there was trouble over parking outside his school so they might be able to help now. Some of the people he talked to didn't know anything about the council. Joe explained that the council was made up of people who were chosen to represent different parts of the town. They all agreed to find out who represented them in their local areas and make a complaint.

1 The skate park is for the use of local people. Who do you think should make decisions about it? Explain why.

2 It is difficult for everyone in the area to be involved in every decision. How could it be made simpler?

3 What kinds of things should people make decisions about in their local area?

Representing everyone

Joe and his friends had an issue that they wanted to discuss: someone in the town had made a decision that they did not like. They wanted to find out who it was and why they had made it. Joe was right when he said they should talk to people on the council as, in this case, the council would have been responsible for the decision.

The local council is made up of local people who make decisions about local services. These **councillors** represent different parts of the town, called **wards**. They are chosen in an election by the people who live in that ward.

In many areas, local elections take place every four years. **Political parties** put forward candidates for people to choose between. Each party will have already decided on a list of plans, called a **manifesto**. These plans will be put into practice if the party wins enough seats on the council.

You will find out how decisions are made about your local area.

Sometimes there is a long list of people to choose from at an election. Some will represent the well-known political parties like Labour, the Conservatives and the Liberal Democrats. Others will represent smaller groups like the Green party, or people who are independent of a party and are campaigning on a local issue. Most councils are a mix of political parties, but the party with most councillors takes overall control.

Almost everyone who is aged 18 or more can vote in these elections. Just like the school council, the process is democratic because everyone can take part. Each year a form is sent to every house in the area to check who is entitled to vote.

Your vote is always secret, so nobody can check on your decision. Has your school or village hall ever been used as a **polling station** on election day?

A polling booth

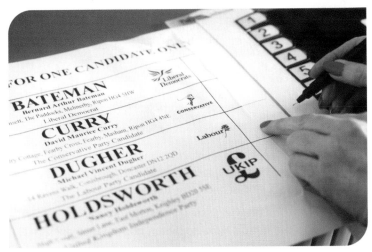

Action

1 Find out who represents your area on the local council.
2 What is the mix of political parties that makes up your local council?
3 Find out about an issue that the council is discussing at the moment. What are the different points of view? Follow it up and find out what happens in the end.

Check your understanding

1 Who is on the local council?
2 How were these representatives chosen?
3 Why are most councils a mix of political parties?
4 Why do you think it is important that your vote is secret?

What's your opinion?

'Local decisions should be made by local people.'
Do you agree with this statement? Give reasons for your opinion, showing you have considered another point of view.

Key Terms

council: a group of people who are elected to look after the affairs of a town, district or county

councillor: a member of a local council, elected by people in that area

manifesto: a published statement of the aims and policies of a political party

political party: an organized group of people with common aims who put up candidates for elections

polling station: a place where votes are cast; often a school, library or village hall

ward: an area that forms a separate part of a local council

How does the council work?

Getting you thinking

Don't close the skate park II

Joe set about finding out how to contact the people at the council who could help with the skate park closure. He rang the main council switchboard and asked to talk to someone who could help him.

He was put through to the Leisure and Recreation department, who said that the council had made the decision because they wanted to use the money to provide better services for the elderly. There had also been some complaints from the neighbours next to the skate park because of the noise, and they were worried about what was going on. Joe was told to contact the member of the council's **cabinet** responsible for leisure. An email or letter might be the best way to make contact because being a councillor is a spare time job; they will be at work during the day.

1 Who makes decisions about local leisure and recreation issues?

2 What differences are there between the councillor and the person who works in the Leisure and Recreation department?

3 Why do you think the council has to make choices between spending money on the skate park and services for the elderly?

4 Why do you think the council takes notice of the people who complain about what goes on at the skate park?

How is the council organized?

Every area of the country elects a councillor. When the council first meets after an election, it elects a leader and the members of the cabinet. The leader and cabinet all come from the political party that won the most votes: they have the **majority**.

Each member of the cabinet will have responsibility for one area of the council's work; for example, education, social services, finance, and leisure and recreation.

Apart from electing the cabinet, the council also elects Overview and Scrutiny committees to make sure the council is run properly.

Being a councillor carries a lot of responsibility, but the role is mainly voluntary. Councillors are paid travel expenses and an attendance fee for meetings, but they don't usually receive a salary.

How does the council do its work?

All the councillors meet to put together the plan for the year. They set the budget for each area of spending. The Overview and Scrutiny committees then make sure this plan is followed.

There are some areas, such as planning for things like housing and road building, that the council as a whole controls. Planning decisions are made according to laws laid down by central government, so the council sets up a committee to make sure that the rules are followed.

All councillors, whether they are members of the cabinet or not, must represent their ward in council decisions. They have a vote in council meetings and must use it in a way that serves their ward best.

As most of the people on the council have full-time jobs, they cannot run the services as well. A **Chief Executive** is appointed to take responsibility for this. In each department, people who are experts in their field are employed to make sure it all runs smoothly.

You will find out how the council does its work.

The structure of the council
The structure shown here is the one that is used most frequently around the UK.

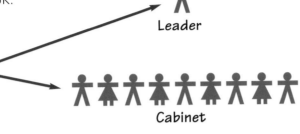

Leader

Members of the political party who won the most seats at the election

Members of the other political parties and groups. Each member is responsible for one area of the local council's work

Cabinet

Council

These people make sure that the council sticks to its plan and budget for each year

Committees

Action
Have a look at your local council's website. Two example addresses are:
   www.suffolkcc.gov.uk
   www.hullcc.gov.uk.
1 How is your council organized? Is there a cabinet and leader?
2 Which political party, if any, has control of your local council?
3 Find out about the work a councillor from your ward does.
4 Who would Joe have to talk to if his skate park was in your area?

Check your understanding
1 What does the council's cabinet do?
2 Who decides how much money to spend on each part of the council's work?
3 What do councillors do for their wards?
4 What's the difference between a councillor and a Chief Executive?

What's your opinion?
'The skate park should stay open.'
Do you agree with this statement? Give reasons for your opinion, showing you have considered another point of view.

What is a mayor?
In most places, a **mayor** has little power but takes part in local ceremonies. When the Queen or other famous people come to visit, the mayor puts on the chain of office and meets them. In May 2002, elections for directly elected mayors were held in a number of towns for the first time.

Key Terms
cabinet: the main decision-making body of the council
Chief Executive: an employee of the council, responsible for the smooth running of services
majority: the party with a majority has won a bigger proportion of the votes than the others
mayor: a member of the council who is selected to be its representative on ceremonial occasions. In some areas they are the elected leader

What does the council do?

Getting you thinking

If all schools looked like this, what effect would it have on:

- the council tax and business rates
- spending on other services that the council provides?

Does your school look like this?

What does the council do?

Your local council is responsible for a range of services for your community, including education, social services, leisure, planning and transport, housing, fire and the police.

The amount of spending will depend on many different things. Here are some examples:

- If the population of the area is very young, they will need lots of schools.
- If there are many old people, they may need help from social services.
- If there are lots of people, there will be lots of refuse to collect.

A brand new sports centre, for example, is a very expensive item that has to be paid for. The council will work out how much it needs to spend in the coming year and then calculate how much money it must raise.

The council funds schools, which are free. It runs sports centres that are usually cheaper than private clubs. The council provides these services because many people would not be able to afford to pay for them otherwise.

Sometimes councils work together with private businesses to run their services. Council houses can be sold to private housing associations, and councils can use the money to repair remaining council property or to build new council housing.

Central government sets a limit on how much money each council can spend. So the council has to work out its priorities. It never has the money to provide everything it would like to. When you vote in local elections, you are helping to decide what happens where you live.

You will discover which services are provided by local government and how the money is raised to provide them.

A local council's income and expenditure (in £ million)

Expenditure

Social services £37.4

Fire and police £8.6

Planning and transport £12.8

Leisure £8.8

Other £6.7

Housing £4.5

Education £62.3

Income

Business rates £45.3

General government grant £26.1

Council tax £68

Tax surplus from last year £1.8

Source: www.statistics.gov.uk

1 Make a list of services provided by this council. Put them in order according to how much they cost.

2 Why does the council spend money on these services?

3 If the council decided to spend more on leisure, where might the money come from?

Action

How does your local council raise and spend its money? You can find out from the town hall, council offices or the library. The council might also have a website with the information.

Check your understanding

1 What sorts of services do local councils provide?
2 Where do local councils get their money from?
3 Why does central government give more money to some councils than others?
4 Why is it important to vote in local elections?

What's your opinion?

'Local taxation should be based on how much you earn instead of the value of your house.'

Do you agree with this statement? Give reasons for your opinion, showing you have considered another point of view.

Where does the money come from?

In order to pay for these services, the local council raises money from residents and businesses in the area. A large part of its spending comes from central government.

Council tax is paid by all the residents of the area. The amount that each person pays will depend on the value of the house they live in. People who live in bigger houses will pay more than those who live in smaller houses.

Business rates are paid by all the local businesses. The amount that is paid depends on the rent that could be charged for the office, shop or factory that the business uses.

Central government contributes a major part. The amount it contributes depends on the needs of the specific area and how much can be raised locally. Poorer areas tend to receive more from central government than richer parts of the country.

Central government helps poorer areas more because it is harder for them to raise money locally. If many people are unemployed, houses will tend to have a lower value, so the council tax will only bring in a relatively small amount of money. Spending in these areas often needs to be greater because people who live there often need a lot of help from Social Services.

Key Terms

business rates: a form of tax paid by all the businesses in an area. The amount a business pays depends on the rent that could be charged for their premises

council tax: a tax paid by everyone who lives in an area. It is based on the value of their house

Talking to the council

Getting you thinking

The Street Café

In Tring, Hertfordshire, a group of school students who are elected members of the **youth council** have quite an effect on what the local council does. Their role is to represent people below the age of 18 in the area. They carried out a survey of young people in the town to find out what they wanted the local council to do for them. The results showed that there was a need for an Internet café where they could meet on a regular basis: and they got one! The Street Café is now up and running and is a regular meeting place for young people in the area.

1 How have the members of the youth council been chosen?

2 Why do people below the age of 18 need to have people to represent them?

3 How have they helped young people in the area?

4 Is there a youth council where you live? Find out from your local council's website. They are easy to find, because they are www.*name of council*.gov.uk

Your views count

In Hertfordshire, the county council takes young people's views seriously. A whole section of its website is aimed at communicating with young people. Not only does it provide lots of information about what's going on, it also has help and advice for young people in the area. And, most important of all, it asks them what they think.

Hertfordshire has youth councils such as the St Albans Youth Council (www.sayc.org.uk) that meet frequently and feed their points of view into the main council. There are many such groups across the county. A young people's web conference has also been used to hear what young people think. The youth councils make an important contribution because under 18s don't have a vote, so their voice isn't heard at an election.

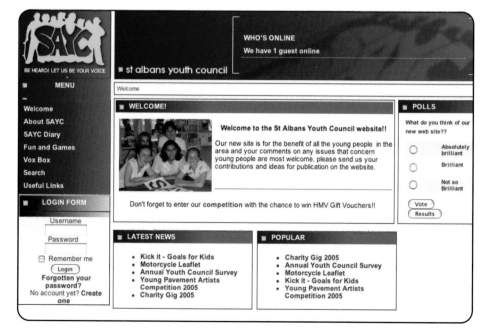

You will find out how people can raise issues with the local council.

Communicating with the council

Everyone's first line of communication with the local council is at the election. Almost all the population aged 18 or over has a vote. The actions of the council between elections will affect people's decisions when it comes to voting.

The way you go about talking to the council will depend on the issue:

- If you want to influence a decision, you need to get to the decision-making process at an early stage. Talking to your councillor is a good start as you can ask advice on how to put across your point of view.
- If you want to find out what is going to happen in the future, ask to look at the **Forward Plan** as this will set out the general aim of the council's plans.
- If you want to find out about a decision that has been made, have a look at the **minutes** of the cabinet meeting.
- If something has gone wrong, you will want to complain. You will probably need to talk to the people employed by the council, but your local councillor will be able to help. If all your complaints fail and you really think the council is in the wrong, you may have to turn to the **ombudsman**. This is the last resort and you need to have done all you can to get the council to sort out the problem.

Action

Look at your local council's website. What does it tell you about getting in touch with people at the council? Does it have a young people's section? If not, ask them why!

Check your understanding

1 How often are council elections held?
2 In which ways could you contact the local council in the following situations?
   - You notice that the paving stones in your street are becoming cracked and uneven.
   - You disagree about plans to build a new supermarket.
   - You want to know how much money is going to be spent on education.
   - You've heard that a youth centre is going to close down.

What's your opinion?

'The local council should take more notice of the views of young people.'
Do you agree with this statement? Give reasons for your opinion, showing you have considered another point of view.

More effective?

A lone voice can sometimes seem too quiet to be heard. A group of people who all have the same views can be more effective than one person campaigning alone. The campaign might be about aircraft noise, wanting a by-pass, not wanting a by-pass, the opening of a new supermarket, the lack of facilities for young people or many, many more issues.

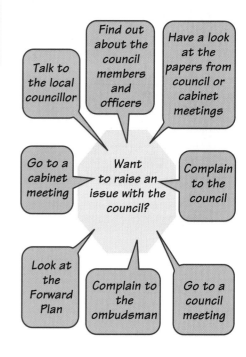

Talk to the local councillor

Find out about the council members and officers

Have a look at the papers from council or cabinet meetings

Go to a cabinet meeting

Want to raise an issue with the council?

Complain to the council

Look at the Forward Plan

Complain to the ombudsman

Go to a council meeting

Key Terms

Forward Plan: a document that sets out the aims of the council in the long term

minutes: a formal record of what has been said at a meeting

ombudsman: a person who investigates complaints against the government or a public organization

youth council: a group of young people who meet to discuss what is going on in the local area and put their ideas to the council

Putting on the pressure

Getting you thinking

I will never forget the day when Jay, a boy from the village, was killed. He wasn't the first person to be hit by a car that was speeding through the village. The council seemed to think that 40mph was quite slow enough, but drivers always thought they could get away with more. What we really needed was a 30mph limit and some rumble strips so everyone noticed.

When Jay died, I realized it was time to act. I started a petition. There were copies in all the local shops, the pub, and with all the local organizations. Soon we had over 5000 signatures and we were ready to make our mark.

I took the advice of our local councillor, who suggested that I should go to the council meeting to make my point. I sent a letter and the petition in advance so they would be prepared. At the meeting I stood up and explained what we were asking for. The council members listened carefully.

The council members understood what we wanted and why we wanted it. Within a few months, we, like other villages, had the 30mph limit that would make our lives safer.

Why was it a good idea to:

1 organize a petition

2 talk to the local councillor

3 send a letter and the petition before the meeting

4 go to the meeting in person?

Pressure groups

People who have a message that they want to get across often form a **pressure group**. A group of people can often have more effect than a single person if they want something to change. Pressure groups want to influence people in government – local, national and even international.

Pressure groups come in all shapes and sizes, but they are usually concerned with one issue or area of policy. For example, the petition for a 30mph limit was started by one person, but in order to put pressure on the local council,

other people got involved. They formed a small pressure group, which had one objective. Once the work was done and the group had succeeded in getting the 30mph limit, they could then stop campaigning.

Many pressure groups work on a much larger scale. Major pressure groups such as Greenpeace and Shelter have objectives that often lead them to put pressure on national government and big businesses, as well as organizing activities at a local level.

You will find out how pressure groups can influence the actions of the council.

> *Is there a group of people who care about the issue?*
> Organize the group and give people responsibilities.

Getting your voice heard

The key to getting your voice heard is to put together a campaign that reaches as many people as possible.

> *Is the message clear?*
> Make sure that everyone understands what you are trying to achieve.

> *Who do you need to talk to?*
> Find out who is responsible for the things you want to change.

> *Have you got good evidence?*
> Do you need a petition to show that lots of people care about the issue? Have you got the facts and figures right?

> *How do you get the message accross?*
> You might give out leaflets in the high street, put out a press release so the local media know what is happening, campaign in public about the issue or prepare a presentation for the council. You will need to fit the method to the audience that you are trying to influence.

> *Can you make your argument more persuasive?*
> Look at all the material you have. Test it out on people. Make sure that the key points are very clear. Are there any key issues which will make people take notice? Use them!

> *Is there a local radio station or newspaper?*
> Local radio stations and papers are always looking for news. How do you get in touch with them?

Action

Is there a local issue that you really care about? Work out what you would do in order to change things.

Check your understanding

1 What is the aim of pressure groups?
2 How can members of a pressure group get their voices heard?
3 Why might a pressure group only exist for a short length of time?

What's your opinion?

'A pressure group is usually more effective than a single person in getting things changed.'
Do you agree with this statement? Give reasons for your opinion, showing you have considered another point of view.

Key Terms

pressure group: a group of people who try to change public opinion or government policy to their own views or beliefs

Getting elected

Getting you thinking

1 What made Jo decide to become an MP?

2 How did Jo decide which political party to join?

3 Why does Jo think people should have their say?

4 What issues do politicians deal with?

5 What could happen if you don't bother to vote?

"Politics has an impact on every aspect of our lives. From protecting our environment, to the quality of your education or how much you get paid for your Saturday job: all of these things are affected by politicians. I decided to stand for election because I wanted to change things, and not just complain about what I didn't like.

I first became interested in politics when I took part in a Parliamentary debate at my secondary school. We took the parts of the government and opposition parties, and throughout the day we debated various issues such as education, health and defence. It was fast and furious. It brought politics to life for me. The issues that I felt particularly strongly about were education and trying to change the way the electoral system works. I joined the Lib Dems when I was a student, mainly because of these two issues. Over time I became interested in other issues such as civil liberties, the environment and the way businesses work with the community.

For a long time I was determined to take up a career in business and keep politics as an interest for my spare time. But when I was first persuaded to stand for Parliament, I began to realize that politics was my real passion. I decided to follow my ambition to represent my home seat in Parliament. Lots of young people don't seem to be interested in politics. But it's all about everyday life, so it's important to vote and play a part. If you don't, you can't really complain about what happens. Becoming an MP means I can really have my say."

Jo Swinson working with young people in her constituency

Becoming a Member of Parliament

There are 659 **Members of Parliament**, or MPs. They have all been elected to represent a part of the country known as a **constituency**. Most MPs were chosen by one of the political parties to be its candidate at an election. If they win the election, they then become the MP who represents everyone in the area.

A few people stand as independents and therefore do not go through the party system. This was the case with a doctor, John Taylor, who was furious that the local hospital was to be closed; he stood as an independent and won the seat.

Map of Birmingham Constituencies

Source: *www.birmingham.gov.uk*

Fighting an election

You have all seen posters everywhere at election time. The campaign starts the minute a **general election** is declared, if not before. The current government tries to choose the best moment to 'go to the country', which is another way of saying 'calling an election'.

To attract voters the political parties and candidates will:

- send out leaflets telling people what they have done in the past and plan to do in future
- go **canvassing**
- attract press coverage
- hold public meetings.

You will discover how an MP gets elected to the House of Commons in order to understand how the electoral system works.

Who shall I vote for?

Whether you decide to vote for the Conservatives, Labour, the Liberal Democrats or one of the smaller parties, all sorts of factors will affect your decision.

Which paper do you read?
Newspapers, radio and TV let people know what's going on but they can also affect how people think. Some newspapers always reflect the ideas of one of the political parties, while others take a wider view.

What's your age, gender and ethnicity?
More young people and ethnic minorities vote Labour. More women used to vote Conservative but the balance has now shifted.

Which social class are you?
Upper and middle class people have tended to vote Conservative and working class people to vote Labour. However, this divide has become less rigid as the parties' policies have become more alike and society has become less class-based.

Do you like the party's policies and image?
People tend to vote for the party as a whole rather than their local candidate. The image of the party and its leader has become increasingly important as the role of the media has increased.

What do your friends think?
People's decisions on who to vote for are often affected by their friends and family.

What's your religion?
Religious beliefs can persuade people to vote for the party that holds views in line with their own.

Where do you live?
Political parties often have strongholds in certain areas. For instance, in the South East, more people have traditionally voted Conservative.

When people have taken all these things into account, they will decide who to vote for. Whoever is elected MP is then responsible for representing all the people in their constituency in Parliament, whichever party they belong to.

Action

1 Who is your local MP? Which political party do they belong to?
2 How many candidates were there at the last election in your constituency? Which parties did they represent? How many votes did they each win?

Check your understanding

1 How many MPs are there in the House of Commons?
2 What is the name for the area represented by an MP?
3 Do all candidates represent one of the main political parties? Explain your answer.
4 How do candidates try to attract voters?
5 What affects how people cast their vote?

What's your opinion?

'I vote for a candidate because my friends and family do.'
Do you agree with this statement? Give reasons for your opinion, showing you have considered another point of view.

Key Terms

canvassing: when people try to persuade others to vote for their party in an election

constituency: the area represented by an MP

general election: an election for a new government. In the UK, these take place at least every five years

Member of Parliament: a person who has been elected to represent a constituency in Parliament

What does an MP do?

Getting you thinking

"Entering the House of Commons for the first time was really exciting. I'd worked so hard throughout the election, so winning my seat was great.

As an MP I hope to make a difference in two ways. Firstly, I can help the 65000 people who live in my constituency. They raise questions and ask me to help sort out their problems at my regular surgeries. They also contact me by letter, telephone or email. I take a keen interest in local issues and get involved in supporting community initiatives.

Secondly, in the House of Commons, we all debate new laws and changes to existing ones. The detailed work on new laws is carried out in committees and not all in the chamber of the House of Commons which you tend to see on television. There are also committees that check up on the work of government departments such as education and health.

I think being an MP is the best job in the world because I can really have an effect on the future of the country."

1 Why was Jo so excited when she entered the House of Commons for the first time?

2 What might you think if you had become an MP and entered the House of Commons for the first time?

3 What did Jo expect to do once she had become an MP?

4 If you had just become an MP, what would you like to change?

Jo Swinson enters the Houses of Parliament for her first day in office.

Taking your seat

For a new MP, taking your seat in the House of Commons is an exciting event. After what might be years of wanting and waiting to be elected, joining the body that runs the country is a big moment.

MPs debate new laws and policies in the House of Commons. Sometimes debates become furious and the **Speaker** has to act very firmly to keep things in order. On occasion, an MP can be temporarily thrown out of the House of Commons if things get out of hand. MPs generally vote with the party to which they belong, but sometimes they follow their conscience.

Starting work

MPs have a range of responsibilities.

Their first responsibility is to the people who elected them. There is often a lot of mail from the constituency, which must be dealt with. An MP will hold a frequent 'surgery' in the constituency to listen to people's ideas and worries. They take part in debates in the House of Commons and will usually vote with their political party.

If they have a post in a government department, they will be busy working on government policy and working out new laws.

They might sit on a committee that keeps a check on the activities of the government departments.

You will discover what Members of Parliament do.

The Speaker is an MP, chosen by the rest to organize business and keep order.

Backbench MPs who don't have jobs in the government or opposition sit on benches at the back.

The government benches: the **Prime Minister** sits at the front surrounded by the **Cabinet**.

The opposition benches: the Leader of the **Opposition** sits at the front, surrounded by the **Shadow Cabinet**.

MPs who don't belong to the main party or largest opposition party also sit on the opposition bench.

Into power

When a political party wins a general election, it forms a government. The leader usually becomes the Prime Minister. His or her first task is to choose the members of the Cabinet. This is the inner circle of people who run the government departments. These departments include:

- the Treasury, which runs the finances
- the Home Department, which is responsible for law and order
- the Foreign and Commonwealth Affairs Office, which is responsible for the UK's interests abroad.

Other departments cover:

- health
- education and skills
- trade and industry
- transport
- culture, media and sport
- international development
- defence
- environment, food and rural affairs.

Wales, Scotland and Northern Ireland also have their own departments.

The people who lead these departments are known as **Secretaries of State**. They have assistants who are called **Ministers of State**. There are also a range of other jobs for non-cabinet MPs in the departments.

After the election, MPs wait for a call from the Prime Minister's office, in the hope of getting a job in the government. Getting the first job in a government department is a step to becoming a Minister.

Check your understanding

1 What is the responsibility of every MP?
2 What does a Secretary of State do?
3 What do government departments do?
4 Who is in the Cabinet?
5 What is the role of the Cabinet?

What's your opinion?

'MPs should always vote with the party they belong to.'
Do you agree with this statement? Give reasons for your opinion, showing you have considered another point of view.

Key Terms

Cabinet: a group of MPs who head major government departments. It meets weekly to make decisions about how government policy will be carried out

House of Commons: the more powerful of the two parts of the British Parliament. Its members are elected by the public

Minister of State: an assistant to the Secretary of State

Opposition: political parties who are not in power

Prime Minister: the leader of the majority party in the House of Commons and the leader of the government

Secretary of State: an MP who is in charge of a government department such as health or defence

Shadow Cabinet: MPs from the main opposition party who 'shadow' MPs who head major government departments

Speaker: the MP elected to act as chairman for debates in the House of Commons

How are laws made?

Getting you thinking

1 Why do you think the Government wanted to make laws like these?

2 What, in your opinion, would happen if the government passed laws that the population did not like?

3 Why do people, in general, keep the laws which are passed by Parliament?

'Ban fox hunting'

'Curfew for teenagers'

'Change the licensing laws'

Power

Parliament passes laws that determine how we live our lives. By electing a government, we give it the power to do this. If people break the laws, they can be punished. The government is given authority (a mandate) because the population accepts that an election is a fair way of deciding who will hold power for a five-year period.

The government is **accountable** because it has to answer to the voters. If voters do not like what is happening, the government will not be re-elected.

How are laws made?

Laws go through several stages before coming into force. The government often puts out a **Green Paper**, which puts forward ideas for future laws. Once the ideas have been made final, a **White Paper** is published.

This lays out the government's policy. To turn policy into law, the proposals are introduced to Parliament in the form of a **bill**. To change the school leaving age, for example, the government would have to introduce an Education Bill. Having gone through the process shown in the diagram on page 81, the bill becomes an **Act** of Parliament and, therefore, part of the law of the country. The government is accountable to the population so it needs to be sure that everyone has had an opportunity to comment.

It is important that laws are carefully put together, or 'drafted', because there are always some people who want to find a way of avoiding them. If a law can be interpreted in a different way, it will be very hard to enforce.

Theme 2: Power, politics and the media

You will understand the process that a bill goes through before it becomes law.

Passing through Parliament

First reading
The bill is introduced formally in the House of Commons. Before it reaches this stage, it has been worked on by a Drafting Committee to make sure that it is correctly put together. A bill can be many pages long. At this stage there is no debate.

Second reading
A few weeks after the first reading stage, the bill is debated fully in the House of Commons. A vote is taken and if the majority of MPs approve of the bill, it is passed.

Standing committee
A group of 16 to 20 MPs look at the bill carefully and make any alterations that came up at the Second Reading, or which they now think are appropriate.

Third reading
The amended bill is presented to the House of Commons. A debate is held and a vote is taken on whether to approve it.

House of Lords
The bill goes through the same process as in the Commons. If the Lords want to change anything, the bill is returned to the Commons.

Report stage
The committee sends a report to the House of Commons with all its amendments. These amendments are either approved or changed. Changes are made when there is a lot of opposition to the bill or if there is strong public pressure to do so.

Royal assent
Once the bill has passed all its stages in the Commons and the Lords, it is sent to the Queen for her signature. This is really a formality, as the Queen would never refuse to sign a bill that had been through the democratic process. The bill then becomes an Act of Parliament and part of the law of the country.

Action

Choose a new law that you would like to see passed. Put your proposals into a 'bill'. Work out what the opposition is likely to say and prepare your arguments.

Check your understanding

1 What is the difference between a bill and an Act?
2 What sort of things do committees have to pay attention to when making amendments to bills?
3 Why do you think there are so many stages before a law is made?

Key Terms

accountable: if you are accountable for something, you are responsible for it and have to explain your actions

Act: a law passed by Parliament

bill: a proposal to change something into law

Green Paper: this puts forward ideas that the government wants discussed before it starts to develop a policy

White Paper: this puts government policy up for discussion before it becomes law

Spending and taxing

Getting you thinking

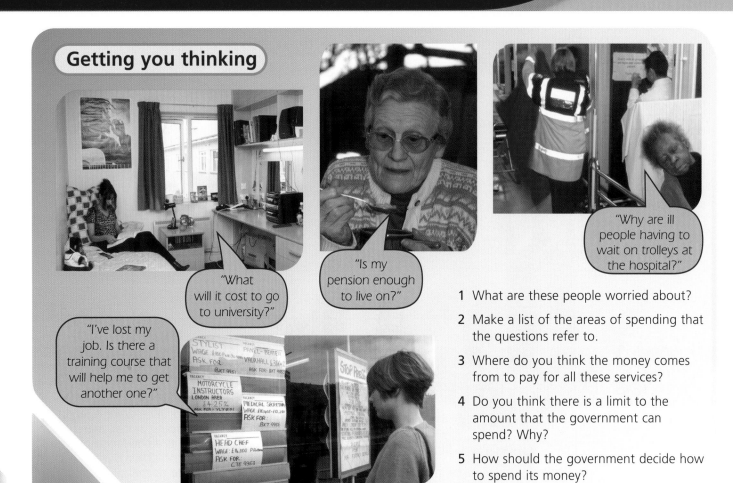

"What will it cost to go to university?"

"I've lost my job. Is there a training course that will help me to get another one?"

"Is my pension enough to live on?"

"Why are ill people having to wait on trolleys at the hospital?"

1 What are these people worried about?

2 Make a list of the areas of spending that the questions refer to.

3 Where do you think the money comes from to pay for all these services?

4 Do you think there is a limit to the amount that the government can spend? Why?

5 How should the government decide how to spend its money?

What does the government spend?

The government spends its money on a wide range of services. The pie chart below shows the main areas of spending and the proportion spent on each area. The way it is divided up varies a little from year to year but the overall picture stays much the same.

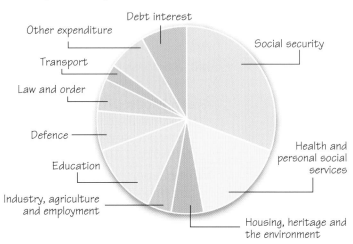

Debt interest
Other expenditure
Transport
Law and order
Defence
Education
Industry, agriculture and employment
Social security
Health and personal social services
Housing, heritage and the environment

Where does the money come from?

If the government is to provide these services, it needs to raise money to pay for them. The money, or **government revenue**, comes from taxation or borrowing as the pie chart below shows.

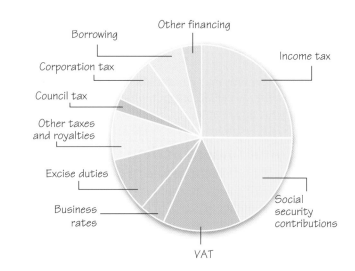

Borrowing
Other financing
Corporation tax
Council tax
Other taxes and royalties
Excise duties
Business rates
Income tax
Social security contributions
VAT

You will find out that the government has to make choices when it spends the money it raises in taxes.

Excise duty is charged on a special range of items, many of which are not very have too much of them. These include alcohol and cigarettes.

Value added tax (VAT) is paid on almost everything we buy, apart from food, children's clothes, books and newspapers. The amount paid is a percentage (17·5%) of the total value of the goods or services.

Corporation tax is paid on the profit made by all businesses.

Other taxes include those on cars and petrol. These allow the government to tax particular items to raise money or to try to reduce the amount we buy. Some taxes are raised in the local area. These include council tax and business rates.

Income tax is not paid by people who earn very little, but as your income rises you pay more tax. It is worked out as a percentage of your earnings. People on high earnings pay a higher percentage of their earnings in income tax.

Making ends meet

The decisions on taxes and spending happen each year in the **Budget**. The **Chancellor of the Exchequer** is responsible for deciding where the money comes from and how it is spent. The Chancellor works with government departments to decide what is needed and what must come first. It can be difficult to get the right balance because often every department will want to spend more.

Just like everyone else, if the government wants to spend more than its income, it has to borrow money. When it borrows, it has to pay interest to the people who lend it the money.

Over the years, there has been a steady increase in the amount that governments spend. At the moment, it amounts to about £6000 per person, per year. People's voting decisions often depend on what the political parties say they will do about taxes and spending if they win the election.

Action

The Treasury is the government department responsible for the Budget. Look at its website at www.treasury.gov.uk to find out how the government raises and spends its money. Click on the 'Budget' heading on the site. You will find a summary document that explains the government's spending decisions.

Check your understanding

1 What does the Chancellor of the Exchequer do? Why can this work be difficult?
2 Explain the different types of taxation that the government uses to raise money.
3 What has been happening to the amount of government spending over the years?
4 Why might government spending influence the way people vote?

What's your opinion?

'If the NHS wants more money, it should get it.'
Do you agree with this statement? Give reasons for your opinion, showing you have considered another point of view.

Key Terms

Budget: the process each year when the Chancellor of the Exchequer explains how the government will raise and spend its money
Chancellor of the Exchequer: the member of the government who is responsible for the country's finances
government revenue: the money raised by the government

Making a difference

Getting you thinking

Cinema complex plans win go-ahead

Detailed plans for a new multi-million pound cinema complex have been approved by town planners.

The decision paves the way for a seven-screen cinema complex and foyer in the heart of Newbury, Berkshire.

The site of the current Market Street car park at the Kennet Centre has been earmarked for the development, which will also include restaurants.

Councillor Sally Hannon said: "The proposed scheme will be a major boost to the vitality of the town.

It will bring economic, social and cultural benefits and greatly enhance the emerging cultural quarter of Newbury.

There has been huge public support for a cinema here, backed by retail studies showing significant need for a modern multiplex in the town."

Source: http://news.bbc.co.uk

Lee says ...

Not having a cinema was a big blow for Newbury and it hit young people very hard, as there wasn't much else to do. If the cinema was to reopen, action was needed. Working with local councillors and the MP, we launched a petition to show how much the town needed a cinema. We got the local press to cover the launch and it was a great success.

Organizing a pressure group campaign with good media coverage taught me how to deal with situations like interviews. It shows prospective employers that I am capable of organizing and carrying out a project. I also felt that I had helped the people of Newbury.

1 Why did Lee decide to help the campaign?

2 How did Lee make a difference?

3 How did Lee's actions help others and himself?

4 Do you decide to join in? If so, what do you do and why?

What do pressure groups do?

Pressure groups often work to promote a cause such as looking after the environment, like the World Wide Fund for Nature and Friends of the Earth, or by helping relieve housing problems, like Shelter. Trade unions and other organizations are pressure groups that work to protect the interest of their members.

How do pressure groups work?

Pressure groups look for the best ways to get their message across and find support. They might:

* use adverts, press releases, special days or media stunts to put an issue in the public eye
* **lobby** MPs by writing to them, meeting them, organizing petitions and trying to involve them in the work of the organization

* try to influence changes in the law
* sponsor MPs and finance political parties.

Lee helped to launch the petition because he felt that he could have an effect and help to get things done. People often say 'they' when referring to government, big business and other organizations which they don't think they can affect: "*They* must do something about ...". Lee decided that *he* could make a difference. He felt that he got something out of it as well. If there's something you feel strongly about, why wait for someone else to do something about it?

You will understand how and why people participate in political parties and pressure groups.

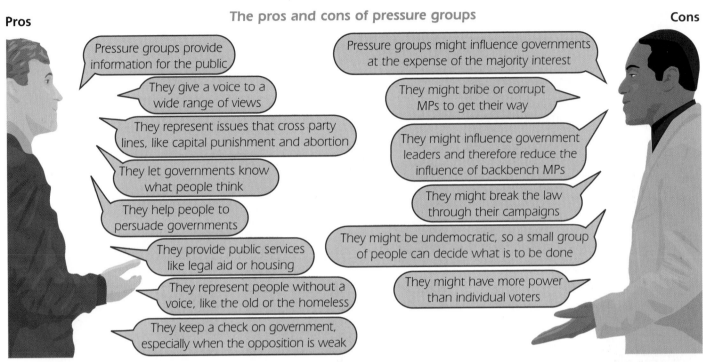

Pros

The pros and cons of pressure groups

Cons

- Pressure groups provide information for the public
- They give a voice to a wide range of views
- They represent issues that cross party lines, like capital punishment and abortion
- They let governments know what people think
- They help people to persuade governments
- They provide public services like legal aid or housing
- They represent people without a voice, like the old or the homeless
- They keep a check on government, especially when the opposition is weak

- Pressure groups might influence governments at the expense of the majority interest
- They might bribe or corrupt MPs to get their way
- They might influence government leaders and therefore reduce the influence of backbench MPs
- They might break the law through their campaigns
- They might be undemocratic, so a small group of people can decide what is to be done
- They might have more power than individual voters

Political parties: why should you join?

If you are interested in politics, you might decide to join the party that holds views closest to your own. The major political parties all have youth sections. Organizations encourage young people to take part because they want people to stay committed to their party later on in life. If you want to find out about them, have a look at their websites, where you will find their manifestos and information about their youth sections.

Greenpeace activists painting the ship 'Agia Irene' which was carrying hundreds of African logs from the last surviving tropical ancient forests

Action

1. Find out about political youth sections from political party websites.
2. Find out about the work of a national or international pressure group. What are their current campaigns? What successes have they had in the past? How do they encourage individuals to join in with their work?

Check your understanding

1. What can individuals do if they want to help shape the way things are done?
2. Why could it be argued that pressure groups help democracy? Why could it be said that they harm democracy?
3. Why are political parties interested in attracting young members?

What's your opinion?

'An individual can have an effect, but you can make a bigger difference if you work with others.'

Do you agree with this statement? Give reasons for your opinion, showing you have considered another point of view.

Key Terms

lobby: to try to persuade MPs to support a particular point of view. This used to happen in the 'lobby', or hallway, on the way into Parliament

More democratic?

Getting you thinking

"But why doesn't Cornwall have a parliament? It's just as different from London as Wales and Scotland."

"I voted for my MP but I wouldn't have voted for that new law that's just been passed!"

"Why should people sit in the House of Lords and make decisions about our future, when they haven't been elected?"

1 Do you think that other regions of the country should have parliaments? Explain your views.

2 Why do we vote for MPs rather than everyone voting for every law that is passed?

3 Do you think that the people in the House of Lords should be elected? Explain your views.

How democratic?

Democracy originated in ancient Athens, Greece, where all citizens voted on every issue. This was less democratic than it sounds because only a small proportion of the population were classed as 'citizens'. Women and slaves, for example, were excluded.

In the UK, we elect MPs to represent us, because the country is too large for everyone to have their say on all occasions. However, MPs vote, in general, according to the policy of their political party. MPs can't vote in a way that suits all their constituents because some voted for another political party and hold different views.

When a **referendum** is held, every voter can make a direct contribution to a decision. In the UK, they are held on topics that have great long-term implications for the country, like joining the Euro. The outcome may be binding or may just be used to advise the government.

Sometimes MPs are given a 'free vote', which means they don't have to vote with their party. Free votes are usually taken on matters of conscience, such as abortion. MPs will often be lobbied hard by pressure groups that want their support. Constituents may also want their MP to vote in a particular way.

Real democracy?

The House of Lords has always had the role of checking and challenging bills as they pass through the system to become law. It has always included **hereditary peers**, who were only there because they had inherited the role. This was not really a good reason for being involved in ruling the country. There has been pressure to reform the House of Lords for a long time.

Life peers, who have been appointed by the government or opposition, also sit in the House of Lords. The number of new life peers is controlled by the government. A number of **people's peers** have also been appointed and there are plans for further change. But the House of Lords is still not really democratic, even though there are now fewer hereditary peers.

Devolution

The Scottish Parliament and Welsh **Assembly** were both set up following referenda. There had been lengthy campaigns for **devolution** in both countries. People wanted devolution because it shifted some power and authority from London to their own capital cities. Scotland voted strongly for its Parliament, which has the ability to raise taxes and pass laws. The Welsh voted by a narrow margin of 0.6% for their Assembly. The Welsh Assembly can spend the UK government's allocation of money to Wales, but it cannot set taxes and make laws because it is not a parliament.

Since the formation of Northern Ireland in 1921, there have been many attempts to create some form of government there. The current Assembly has powers to control education, health and local government, but the Assembly has often been suspended because of disagreement among Irish politicians.

There are calls for regional assemblies in the rest of the UK too. Many people in regions such as Cornwall feel that their part of the country is distinctive and has different needs from the rest of the UK. People in the North East, however, rejected the idea when a referendum was held. The cost of running a regional assembly was one factor in their decision.

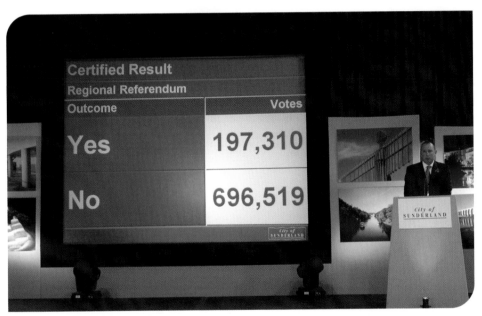

Certified Result
Regional Referendum

Outcome	Votes
Yes	197,310
No	696,519

Check your understanding

1 What is the purpose of a referendum? When are they held?
2 What kind of issues are MPs allowed a free vote on? Why?
3 Who can influence MPs when they have a free vote?
4 What's the difference in the amount of power held by the Scottish Parliament and the Welsh Assembly?
5 Why do some people want to have regional governments?

What's your opinion?

'Devolution means that better decisions are made for a region because they are made locally.'
Do you agree with this statement? Give reasons for your opinion, showing you have considered another point of view.

Key Terms

Assembly: a body of people elected to decide on some areas of spending in a region

devolution: the transfer of power from central to regional government

hereditary peers: people who inherited the title 'Lord' or 'Lady'

people's peers: people who are selected to sit in the House of Lords

referendum: a vote by the whole electorate on a particular issue

Vote, vote, vote!

Getting you thinking

Old enough to pay taxes but not to decide which politicians should spend them.

Old enough to get married and have kids but not to vote on education policy.

Old enough to serve your country but not to elect the people who make the decisions.

IT'S TIME 16 YEAR OLDS WERE TREATED AS ADULTS

VOTE AT 16

We make a valuable contribution to society – but we can't . . . .

vote

Join **Votes at 16** now

For further information contact
E-mail info@votesat16.org.uk and www.votesat16.org.uk

The National Youth Agency
www.nya.org.uk

1 What's your reaction to the poster? Do you agree that 16-year-olds should be allowed to vote?

2 Think of arguments you would add to the ones in the poster if you were trying to persuade someone that 16-year-olds should be given the vote.

Threats to democracy?

In the 2005 General Election, only 60% of the **electorate** voted. The Labour Party won 55% of the seats in the House of Commons with only 35% of the votes. Some say that this means the United Kingdom is no longer a very democratic country.

Making your vote count

'First past the post' is the system used for general elections in the UK. People have one vote in one constituency and the candidate with the most votes in each constituency becomes the MP for that area.

If you added all the votes in the country together, sometimes the winning party does not have the most votes. In each constituency, the candidate with the most votes wins, whether the majority is small or large. If the party that wins the most seats has lots of small majorities, the total vote count may be smaller than that of the opposition.

When all the constituencies in the country are taken together, the proportion of the votes each party won

might not be the same as the proportion of seats each party has in the government. This also makes it hard for small parties to win any seats.

A new system of voting?

Proportional representation, or PR, means that every vote counts. Northern Ireland uses the single transferable vote system (STV) of PR. The constituencies are larger, so each one elects five or six people. Voters put all the candidates in order of preference, putting 1 against their favourite candidate, 2 against their second favourite, and so on. Candidates with the most votes overall win their seats in government.

One issue: one vote

In a referendum you vote on a particular issue, so people really feel that they can have an effect. This might encourage more people to vote because they can pick and choose the policies they agree with. It is, however, very difficult for a government to plan if referenda are held on every topic.

You will develop an understanding of the ways in which people might be encouraged to vote in the UK.

Persuading people to vote

Party political broadcasts

During the 2005 general election, about 50% of the population watched party political broadcasts compared with 70% in 1997. In future, it is thought that short American style election adverts might interest more voters.

The Internet

Political parties could use the Internet to provide information and organize online surveys of public opinion. People might want to vote if they could join in debates and had easier access to information.

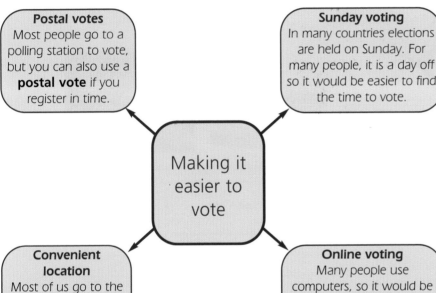

Postal votes
Most people go to a polling station to vote, but you can also use a **postal vote** if you register in time.

Sunday voting
In many countries elections are held on Sunday. For many people, it is a day off so it would be easier to find the time to vote.

Making it easier to vote

Convenient location
Most of us go to the supermarket, so why not use them as polling stations?

Online voting
Many people use computers, so it would be quick and easy to use them to vote, whether you were at home or at work.

Kate Ford of Coronation Street announced that she votes for the Green Party. Are celebrity voters another way to attract others?

Check your understanding

1. Why might low voter turnout be a bad thing for democracy?
2. What does 'first past the post' mean? How does it affect small parties?
3. Why might proportional representation be a fairer system than 'first past the post'?
4. Comment on the different ways of helping increase participation in elections. Do you think they would be successful? Are there any disadvantages? Give reasons.
5. Plan your own campaign to attract young voters and present it to the class.

What's your opinion?

'People should be able to vote at 16.'
Do you agree with this statement? Give reasons for your opinion, showing you have considered another point of view.

Key Terms

electorate: all those registered to vote

first past the post: an electoral system where voters have one vote per constituency and the candidate with the most votes wins

postal vote: when voters make their vote by post, rather than by going to a polling station

proportional representation: an electoral system in which the number of seats a party wins is roughly proportional to its national share of the vote

What is the media?

Getting you thinking

1 Write a sentence for each of these examples of the **media**, explaining how you use them.

2 Put them into groups that show their main use, for example, 'entertainment' and 'information'.

3 Do you believe or trust more of what you learn from one kind of media than from another? Draw up and complete the table with examples of the media.

4 How do you decide what to trust?

5 What effect does reading, seeing or hearing material that you don't trust have on your views?

Media	I trust everything	I trust most things	I trust some things	I trust very little
Newspapers				
TV				
Radio				

Mass media

The media has become a massive industry during the last 50 years. One hundred years ago, newspapers were the only form of information about what was happening in people's locality, the UK and beyond. In days when many people couldn't read, they only knew what people told them.

Today, there is information on every corner in the form of newspapers and magazines. Television is available 24 hours a day. Cable television and the digital revolution have changed things even more. They provide news, entertainment and education whenever you want it, even from your mobile phone.

Viewers, listeners and readers

Habits change. A hundred years ago, politicians could expect to speak to a packed hall at election time. There

was no television, so it was the only way people could ever see who they were voting for. Today, the numbers watching party political broadcasts are in decline. Perhaps there is so much exposure that people are no longer curious about who governs them.

As new methods of communication arrive, people move on. When radio was introduced, families would sit around it listening carefully. When television broadcasts started, radio listening declined. Now we have over 50 television channels, so each company has to work extra hard to attract our attention. With more families having the Internet at home, television watching may decline. What will come next?

You will develop an understanding of the scope and influence of the media.

Who does what?

Despite all the changes, people still buy newspapers, books and magazines, listen to the radio and watch television. The choice of media means that we select the ways of finding out information which suit us best. Although the patterns change, most people use most media most of the time. They simply adjust the amount of time they spend on each one.

Adult participation in selected leisure activities (%): by age							
Age	16–19	20–24	25–29	30–44	45–59	60–69	70+
Watching TV	100	99	99	99	99	99	99
Listening to radio	92	93	93	92	89	82	76
Listening to records/tapes	98	97	95	91	83	71	57
Reading books	63	67	66	65	67	64	64

Source: Social Trends 2005, ONS

The Internet

Political parties could use the Internet to provide information and organize online surveys of public opinion. People might want to vote if they could join in debates and had easier access to information.

Action

1 Look at a range of papers from the same day. Do they tell the stories in different ways? How are they different?
2 Watch the news on television on the same day. Does it give the same picture? Do different channels take a different approach?
3 Do you prefer one newspaper's or television channel's way of telling the story? Do you believe one more than the other? Explain why.

Check your understanding

1 What is meant by the media?
2 How has the media changed over the last 100 years?
3 What does the media provide?
4 Why is the media powerful?

What's your opinion?

'Newspapers are more powerful now than they were a hundred years ago.'
Do you agree with the statement? Give reasons for your opinion, showing you have considered another point of view.

Products for people

All forms of media aim to provide what the customer wants. There are television channels that are aimed at young people and others at an older population.

There is also a growing number aimed at people with specific interests, ranging from music to gardening and cooking to history.

A source of power?

Giving people information can be a source of power. The decision about what to tell and what not to tell means that you can affect the way people think. When people vote in an election, they are making decisions that affect the country for the next five years. How do they make their voting decisions? Very often, they are based on information from the media. The media therefore helps people to make decisions. If it is not accurate, the effect can be very damaging. If the media presents what it wants people to know, rather than the whole truth, it is difficult for people to make informed decisions.

The following pages explore reasons why the media does not always present the whole truth and why the freedom to communicate is important for democracy.

> ### Key Terms
> media: ways of communicating with large numbers of people

Why should the press be free?

Getting you thinking

Journalists protest in Namibia about the clampdown on press freedom in Zimbabwe, the country next door. They would have been arrested if they had protested in Zimbabwe.

ZIMBABWE
Laws passed that:

- only allow foreign journalists into the country to cover specific events
- only allow registered journalists to work
- require media organizations to be registered
- stop people criticizing the President
- limit publication of important information
- stop stories that discriminate against a political party
- only allow demonstrations that have government approval.

International journalist arrested

The Independent newspaper's Zimbabwe reporter has been arrested under new laws. His house had been ransacked and he was told that the order for his arrest had come from the highest level in the government.

"The worst-ever attack on the liberties of the people."

A member of the Zimbabwean parliament

Zimbabwe was about to have an election when these laws were passed.

1 What did these laws prevent?

2 Why do you think the government brought them into force?

3 What effect do you think this had on the results of the election?

4 Explain why the laws were seen as "the worst-ever attack on the liberties of the people".

5 Why is it important for the media to be free to report on events?

6 Do you think there should be any limit on what the media can say?

What is freedom?

'Everyone has the right to the freedom of opinion and expression; this right includes freedom to hold opinions without interference and to seek, receive and impart information and ideas through any media, regardless of frontiers.'

Universal Declaration of Human Rights

One of every human being's rights is to have their say. If they don't like the government, they should be free to say so. If people think the government should spend more or less on health, education or defence, laws should not prevent them from saying so. If people want to know what is going on, they should be free to find out. Information and data should not be kept secret unless there is a good reason. In a democracy, people need to be able to hear others' points of view and know what is going on if they are to use their vote effectively.

You will understand the importance of a free press.

Why control the press?

If information is kept from people, they will find it hard to decide whether the government is keeping its promises or breaking the law in order to stay in power. If a government is determined to stay in power, preventing people from knowing the truth can be very effective. **Censorship** means that people will only know what you want them to know.

Press freedom is often the first thing to go when the government of a country wants to prevent democracy working. A country that controls the press cannot really be democratic. There are examples throughout history. In the last century, the Soviet Union controlled all forms of media. Even today, there are no television channels that are free from government control in Russia, as part of the former Soviet Union is now known. China also has strong controls on what the people are told. There are examples of press control throughout the world.

A voter in Zimbabwe reading a government-owned paper which accuses the opposition party of terrorism. All media output is controlled by the government.

In Russia the government controls all television output.

Is it ever right to control the media?

When the UK was fighting Argentina over the Falkland Islands in 1981, there was a complete news blackout. Every night a government spokesman appeared on the television and gave a report. He read a message in a slow, serious manner, telling us what the government thought we should know.

When people are caught spying, very often much of the information that is provided in court is not published.

These are both examples of occasions when national security is thought more important than press freedom. Sometimes, by telling people everything, you may be giving the game away. There is, however, always a debate about how much information should be given out.

Check your understanding

1 What does the Universal Declaration of Human Rights have to say about press freedom?
2 Why might a government that wants to be re-elected decide to control the press?
3 Why can democracy not work effectively if the press is controlled?
4 Are there reasons why press freedom should sometimes be limited? Why?
5 Draw up a list of issues that you think the press should be free to discuss and any that you think it should not be allowed to print stories about. Use your list to draw up a law on press freedom.

What's your opinion?

'The media must always be free to express a point of view.'
Do you agree with this statement? Give reasons for your opinion, showing you have considered another point of view.

Key Terms

censorship: limiting the information given to the general public

press freedom: the ability of the press to give information and express opinions without control

2.2: The media

93

Legal, decent, honest and truthful?

Getting you thinking

1 Identify the different sorts of people in these pictures.

2 What sorts of thing does the press do to give people cause for complaint?

3 Do you think that complaints are always justified?

4 Make a list of things you feel the press should not do.

5 Make suggestions about how to stop the press doing this sort of thing.

What are the rules?

Anyone in the public eye can be pestered by the press. People find themselves being looked at through the long lens of a camera and on the front page the next day. Ordinary people who have had some good luck or experienced misfortune are just as vulnerable as the famous.

The Press Complaints Commission attempts to prevent this invasion of privacy but it is not always successful. It has drawn up the **Press Code** as guidance for **journalists** working in the media. Although it can look at complaints and decide if the code has been broken, it can do little to prevent it happening again.

The wrong side of the law?

Sometimes it's a question of invading people's privacy, but on other occasions the media gets its facts wrong. When this happens, a paper or television channel can find itself in court facing a **libel** or **slander** case.

Laws prevent anyone from making public statements about people that are not true. Footballers have challenged people who said they fixed a game, politicians have challenged newspapers that said they received money for asking particular questions in Parliament. Private Eye, the magazine that takes a satirical look at the world, often finds itself in court because it has pushed the limits too far.

The Press Code

Newspapers:
- must not publish inaccurate, misleading or distorted information or pictures
- must give a right to reply to any inaccurate reporting
- must respect people's private and family life
- must not harass people for information
- must not intrude on grief or shock
- must not intrude on children during their schooling
- must not use hidden bugs to find things out
- must avoid prejudice
- must not make payments to people involved in criminal cases
- must not profit from financial information
- must not identify victims of sexual assault
- must protect confidential sources

You will find out how rules about what can and cannot be published are enforced.

Popular or quality?

People buy four times more popular papers than quality papers. The quality press tends to take a more serious view of the world and their headlines reflect this. In contrast, on days when dramatic world events are taking place, popular papers have been famous for headlining footballers, sex and money.

Average sales of daily newspapers in the UK

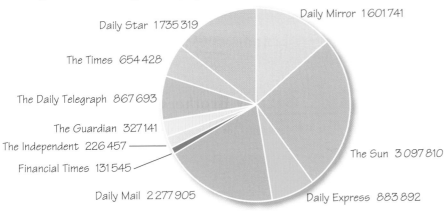

- Daily Star 1 735 319
- The Times 654 428
- The Daily Telegraph 867 693
- The Guardian 327 141
- The Independent 226 457
- Financial Times 131 545
- Daily Mail 2 277 905
- Daily Mirror 1 601 741
- The Sun 3 097 810
- Daily Express 883 892

Legal limits

Just like anyone else, the media has to obey laws about decency. Discrimination is against the law and some parts of the media have to be very careful not to overstep the limits.

The popular papers find themselves in front of the Press Complaints Commission or in court more often than the quality press. But who is responsible? After all, the more sensational the story, the more we want to buy the paper.

Action

1 What decisions has the Press Complaints Commission made recently? Do you agree with their findings? Why?
2 Look at the headlines on a range of newspapers on the same day. How do the popular and quality papers compare? You will find newspapers on the Internet as well as in newsagents.

Check your understanding

1 How should people's privacy be protected?
2 How effective do you think the Press Complaints Commission is?
3 Can you think of any examples when their rules have been broken?
4 Why is it important for journalists to protect confidential sources of information?
5 How do quality papers differ from the popular papers?
6 How does the law limit what newspapers can print?

What's your opinion?

'Celebrities work hard to attract media attention but they should be protected when the press invades their privacy.'

Do you agree with this statement? Give reasons for your opinion, showing you have considered another point of view.

Key Terms

journalist: a person who gathers news and produces reports for the media

libel: writing incorrect things about people

Press Code: guidelines for the media and journalists about the information they gather and how they obtain and use it

slander: saying incorrect things about people

What news?

Getting you thinking

Who owns the papers?

1 Which media company owns the most papers?

2 Which companies also have a share in television companies?

3 If the people who run the companies have strong views, what effect might this have on the news in the papers and on television?

4 Why do you think the government limits the number of papers and television stations that can be owned by one company?

News Corp
The Times Sunday Times The Sun
News of the World A large part of BSkyB

Trinity Mirror
The Mirror Sunday Mirror
The People

Guardian News Group
The Guardian The Observer

Independent News & Media
The Independent The Independent on Sunday

Daily Mail & General Trust
Daily Mail Mail on Sunday
London Evening Standard Metro
20% share of Independent Television News

Barclay Brothers
The Daily Telegraph The Telegraph on Sundays

Where does the power lie?

A newspaper or television news programme can choose the stories it wants to tell. It can also decide how to tell the story. The owners of a paper appoint an **editor** to run it for them. The editor has the power to make these decisions. Often, an editor is chosen because they have the same points of view as the owners: so the way the news is presented reflects the owner's point of view. Television news has editors too. They put the programme together in just the same way.

Most newspapers are in the hands of companies that are owned by shareholders. The objective is to make a profit, so sales are a top priority. And lots of sales means lots of advertising. Businesses that want to sell their products will buy space in papers with many readers. A large proportion of the costs of running a paper are covered by selling space for advertising. Commercial television is just the same.

All these factors combine to make newspapers and television very powerful.

Who buys what?

Most people read a paper that agrees with their own views. Conservative voters often buy The Daily Telegraph or The Express, while Labour voters might buy The Guardian or Daily Mirror. The way the news is presented depends on the views of the papers. The cartoons are often the give-away. They are always ruder about the party they don't support!

The influence of advertising

Advertising pays for commercial television and the papers. What would you do if, as editor, you were faced with a story that showed one of your main advertisers in a bad light?

Would you:

- run the story?
- hold it for a day when there were no adverts from that business?
- rewrite the story so it was less critical?
- just ignore it?

It's a tough decision to make.

In a spin?

Politicians often want to be at the top of the news and shown in a good light. Political parties employ **spin doctors** who write the stories and work hard to get them in the news. A common story is about new government spending on health, education or other areas that people care about. When journalists look carefully, however, they often find that the spending has been announced several times before! This is often the work of spin doctors.

Whose views?

Everyone has a point of view, and often it is hard to hide. If, as a reader or viewer, you are aware of the **bias** of a television programme or newspaper, you can take it into account. If not, you may just believe it all. In a country where only one point of view is permitted, people are unlikely to know what is really going on.

Under control

Every time one media company wants to take over another, the plans are reviewed. If the takeover puts too much power in too few hands, it won't be allowed to go ahead. When Granada bought United's television stations, it was told that HTV would have to be sold, otherwise Granada would have had too much power.

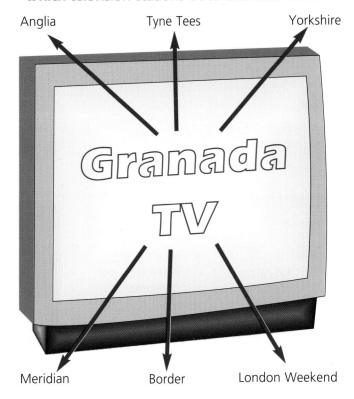

Which television stations does Granada own?

Anglia · Tyne Tees · Yorkshire · Meridian · Border · London Weekend

Action

Compare articles about the same story or event in two different newspapers. Is there a difference in the way the stories are told? Is there any bias?

Check your understanding

1 What does an editor do?
2 Why are media owners powerful?
3 What factors influence the contents of a newspaper?
4 How is media ownership controlled?

What's your opinion?

'Media owners have too much influence on the way we think.'
Do you agree with this statement? Give reasons for your opinion, showing you have considered another point of view.

Key Terms

bias: to favour one thing over another unfairly

editor: the person who is responsible for the content of a newspaper or television or radio programme

spin doctor: someone who tries to get certain stories into the public eye and to make bad news sound better

TV: information or entertainment?

Getting you thinking

1 Which channels do you think the man is most likely to be looking for? Why?

2 Draw up a pie chart showing the different sorts of television you watch. Explain your choices.

3 Do you think the TV programmes you watch influence how you think about issues?

4 What would persuade you to change your viewing habits?

What's on the telly?

Most people have four or five television channels to watch. A rapidly increasing number have 100 or more channels. The introduction of satellite, cable and freeview television has shifted people's viewing patterns considerably. If you want to watch sport or cartoons all day, you can! Equally, if you want to watch what's going on in Parliament all day, you can do that too.

All the television channels are in competition with each other. Ones with advertising have to show they have lots of viewers if they are to sell advertising time. The BBC is funded by the licence fee. We pay to watch it, but questions are asked if viewing figures fall. As viewing numbers are so important, television companies will put out the programmes that they think lots of people want to see.

More channels mean more opportunities for specialist interests because production costs are falling. Nickleodeon,

Which one will you watch? Why?

for example, comes from an office in a side street in London. All it needs is a small studio and the ability to run recorded programmes.

All this airtime can have several effects:
- minority interests can be catered for
- information can be provided in different ways for different people
- quality falls because channels have to fill the time.

TV channel of choice: by age - United Kingdom (%)					
	16–24	25–44	45–64	65 and over	All aged 16 and over
BBC One	26	31	40	47	36
ITV1	20	29	26	25	26
Channel 4 (S4C in Wales)	12	7	6	5	7
BBC Two	6	4	6	10	6
Sky Sports	12	3	2	2	4
Five	2	4	3	3	3
Sky One	5	4	1	1	3

Source: Social Trends 2005, ONS

Great Britain	percentages			
	16 – 24	25 – 64	65+	All aged 16+
News	83	94	97	93
Factual	69	87	84	84
Drama	75	80	87	81
Entertainment	89	76	70	77
Regional	50	72	85	71
Current affairs	57	68	79	68
Educational	45	61	52	57
Sports	51	54	53	53
Arts	30	33	43	35
Children's	41	33	17	31
Religious	11	19	51	24

Interest in television programme type: by age
Source: Independent Television Commission, Ofcom

What goes on in Parliament?

Television cameras are allowed in the Houses of Parliament. Rules were set up about where the cameras were put, who could be filmed and what was to be avoided. For instance, they are not allowed to film an MP who has fallen asleep during a long debate! Output is carefully monitored to give 'a balanced, fair and accurate' picture of the views of all political parties.

When broadcasting began, there was lengthy coverage and few people watched. There are still daily, live programmes but it is now used mainly for news highlights and special events.

Two websites, cable and satellite TV have continuous coverage. These are mainly watched at moments when big issues are being debated and by people who have particular interests in the day's events. It gives access to the UK's Parliament to people all round the world.

The whole story?

Almost everyone can vote at 18. Which box to tick on a ballot paper is an important decision because your vote will help to determine the party that controls the country for the next five years. How will you decide? Will you be influenced by what your friends do? By what your parents say? Or will you think about it and come to your own decision?

Television and radio can help you to know what's going on so you can make a decision for yourself. Listening to both sides of a discussion will help you to decide. Only 1% of terrestrial television's output is news, politics or about what's happening to the economy. Viewing figures among the young are low.

Action

When you watch television tonight, make a note of all the incidents that refer to issues relating to Citizenship.

Check your understanding

1 What are the advantages of having more television channels?
2 How does the pattern of TV watching differ between the young and old? Why do you think this is so?
3 Why do you think there is so little coverage of news and current affairs on the television?
4 How can television and radio help you to decide who to vote for?
5 Why do you think it is important for television coverage of Parliament to be 'balanced, fair and accurate'?

What's your opinion?

'Young people should watch more news and current affairs on the television.'
Do you agree with this statement? Give reasons for your opinion, showing you have considered another point of view.

What's the message?

Many television programmes have information that is useful for Citizenship. For example, there is plenty of material on sustainable development (see page 128). The workings of business and the economy are often part of the story in drama programmes. Even soaps can help you to think about how communities work. They often help you to understand because they show you real situations where people are affected by what's going on.

Can you say what you like?

Getting you thinking

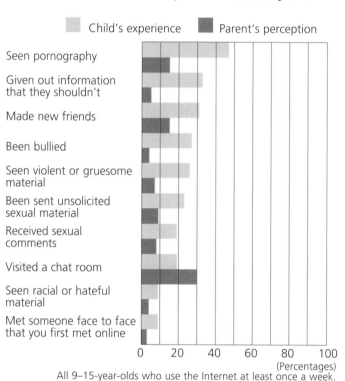

Do children do what their parents think they do?

Child's experience   Parent's perception

- Seen pornography
- Given out information that they shouldn't
- Made new friends
- Been bullied
- Seen violent or gruesome material
- Been sent unsolicited sexual material
- Received sexual comments
- Visited a chat room
- Seen racial or hateful material
- Met someone face to face that you first met online

0   20   40   60   80   100
(Percentages)

All 9–15-year-olds who use the Internet at least once a week.

Source: 'UK Children Go Online', London School of Economics (www.children-go-online.net)

1 Why can ease of access to the Internet mean that people might be shocked by what they see?

2 Do you think anyone should be able to put anything on the Internet? If not, what, in your opinion should be controlled?

3 If material on the Internet is controlled, are there situations in which people might not get the information they need to make decisions, for example, during elections?

Find out – about anything?

There is little to prevent anyone putting anything on the web. It is often hard to track just where material comes from. You will be in trouble, however, if you download information that breaks the law of the country where you live. People's use of the Internet has been used to prove their guilt in all sorts of cases, from terrorism to paedophilia. Even at work, staff have been sacked for breaking the rules on downloading unacceptable materials and sending the wrong sort of emails.

All laws about what can and can't be published in other media apply to material on the Internet, providing the source of information can be tracked.

Free access?

The **Freedom of Information Act** allows everyone to see their personal records. It also means that information held by public bodies should be available. There is already a great deal of government information available on the web. Every government department and local authority has its own website to inform the population about what is going on. But remember, whatever you see on the web may be there to persuade you rather than just give you information.

You will consider whether the Internet should be censored.

Free for all?

Many websites started out by offering free services to their visitors. Once people had grown used to using them, many started to charge for the service. The Times, for example, used to allow free access to all past newspapers but now, if you want to download an article, there is a charge. As the web moves on, charging for information that people really want is likely to become more common.

The Internet for citizens

People need to be informed if they are to participate. The Internet can provide information, ideas, views and opportunities to discuss. All the political parties have their own websites, and broadcasters can keep you up to date on what's going on.

In countries where information isn't free, the Internet can help people to know what is going on in the rest of the world. In some countries where the government really wants to limit information, they limit Internet access.

Households with Internet access in Britain

1999	10%
2000	19.5%
2003	44%

Social Trends 2005, ONS

1 What is happening to the number of households with Internet access?

2 If this continues, how might it affect the way information is communicated to the world?

China's solution

In China, the government works hard to control access to the Internet. All content providers must register with them and are issued with a licence if their material is acceptable. The government has strict rules about religious and political information. There are harsh penalties for anyone who breaks the rules.

In China, access to the Internet is strictly controlled.

Action

Choose a website you would like to know more about and decide how reliable it is. Who wrote it? Is it up-to-date? Is there any bias?

Check your understanding

1 What are people not allowed to put in print? Look back at previous pages.
2 How can access to the Internet be controlled?
3 How is the use of material on the Internet controlled?
4 How can a country limit access to the Internet?
5 How can the Internet help people to be more informed citizens?

What's your opinion?

'People should be free to put whatever they want on the Internet.' Do you agree with this statement? Give reasons for your opinion, showing you have considered another point of view.

Know what you're looking at

Not all websites are quite what you think they are. Some people want to influence the views of others by putting convincing-looking information on the web. The motive may be to persuade people to accept or believe in their views. Unless you are careful, you can be taken in.

Key Terms

Freedom of Information Act: a law that gives open access to information about individuals, business and government

Whose views?

Getting you thinking

My friends think...

I found it on the Internet...

But Dad, I read it in the Sun...

But I saw it on TV...

1 How are all these people making decisions?

2 What problems are there in making decisions in these ways?

3 Do you think there are better ways of making decisions?

4 Draw some bubbles with statements which you think might help them to make more informed decisions.

Subject to persuasion?

We are all subject to persuasion, but we need to look in the right places to be persuaded. People very often read the newspaper that agrees with their views and switch channels on TV when they hear messages that contradict their own ideas. They don't even hear the other side of the story.

There are all sorts of decisions that are made about where you live, your school life or your social life. If the decisions are to be sensible, there are all sorts of points of view that need to be taken into account. Remember Joe, on page 66, who wanted to fight the council when it closed the skate park? The council had listened to the neighbours who complained about the noise and the people who wanted to spend more money on other things, but it hadn't consulted the users of the skate park.

Stories like this are often reported in the local paper. Can you imagine what it would be like if the press could only report the council's point of view and nobody was allowed to challenge it? What effect would this have on people's views?

What information?

More and more information is available to us. The government collects masses of data that are put together by the Office of National Statistics. You'll find lots on its website. The Freedom of Information Act also allows access to a wide range of information about people, businesses and government.

The **Data Protection Act**, however, prevents information that is stored on computers being given out freely. The Human Rights Act may limit information that can be published about people.

There is a balance between helping people to find information and limiting the information that is available, to protect privacy or the national interest.

You will investigate how people are influenced.

Opinions for the public?

The media is full of **opinion polls**. Questions are asked about all sorts of topics from love to politics. When elections are looming, pollsters are out in force and the results of their surveys are published almost daily. "Are voters changing their minds?" is the first thought of many journalists.

The use of opinion polls has been questioned. If one party, according to the polls, is very popular, its supporters might not vote on election day because they may assume enough people will vote anyway. The party that is behind often fears that more voters will desert the sinking ship. If a poll shows that the parties are very close, it can be misleading because it is hard to get it exactly right.

In some countries, these fears have led to the publication of opinion polls being banned in the last weeks before an election.

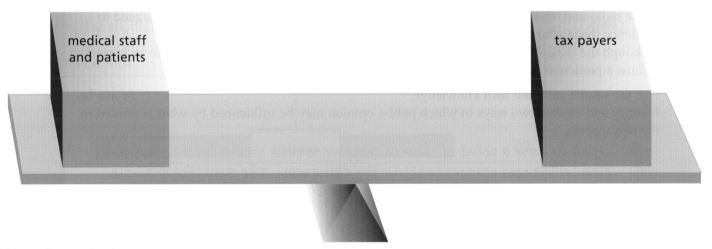

Keeping a balance

Whenever people have to come to a decision, they need to listen to a variety of points of view. These are often talked of as the views of **stakeholders**, or people who have an interest in the decision. If you ask, "Should the government spend more on health?" you have to think about the patients and medical staff, as well as the people who will receive less funding or the tax payer who will pay more tax. They are all stakeholders.

A search through the media often provides the material you need to decide for yourself.

Action

Find an opinion poll that has been carried out recently. What are the results? Does it influence your views? Explain why or why not.

Check your understanding

1 If the local council wants to build a new road to bypass a local shopping area, who should it consult?
2 How does restricting press freedom affect people's views?
3 What is an opinion poll?
4 Why can opinion polls be a) helpful, b) misleading?
5 Why do you need to consider the views of stakeholders?

What's your opinion?

'I know what I think and no one will change my mind.'
Do you agree with this statement? Give reasons for your opinion, showing you have considered another point of view.

Key Terms

Data Protection Act: a law that limits the way that information stored on computers can be used

opinion poll: questioning a sample of the population to build a picture of the views of the public on a particular topic

stakeholder: someone who has an interest in a decision that is being made

5. Identify two ways in which MPs can find out about the problems and concerns of people in their constituency. *(2 marks)*

> MPs hold a surgery in their constituency. Members of the public, whichever party they voted for, can come to ask about their problems. They can also find out through stories in the press or TV.

You might have other ideas too. MPs usually have their own website to tell constituents about what they are doing. A constituent might send an email to them.

6. Give one reason for and one reason against changing the way MPs are elected to the House of Commons. *(2 marks)*

> For: Sometimes the party that forms the government is not the one with the most votes across the country.
>
> Against: The first past the post system gives strong government as parties usually get big enough majorities to run the country.

You might also have said that people like the system because it has single member constituencies so their MP really represents them.

You might also have said that the system means that many people's votes are wasted because they live in constituencies with big majorities for the other party.

Source: Edexcel Citizenship Studies 2003, 2004

Extended writing

"The voting age should be reduced to 16."

Do you agree with this statement?

Give reasons for your opinion, showing that you have considered another point of view.

You could include the following points in your answer and other information of your own.

• What are the rights and responsibilities of a 16-year-old?

• Do their rights and responsibilities justify having a vote?

• Will it help turnout and participation?

• Do 16-year-olds have enough experience of life and maturity to vote?

• Will it make government more representative of the population?

Source: Edexcel Citizenship Studies 2003

At 16 people can smoke, play the lottery, join the army and get married so they should be able to vote. They pay taxes too because there is VAT on almost everything they buy. If they can't vote, they don't have a say in how this money is spent by the government. All these rights and responsibilities mean that people should be able to vote at 16.

Turnout in elections has been falling over the last few elections so giving the vote to 16 year olds will help to increase this. People are not interested in politics because politicians don't seem to take any notice of what we think. Perhaps if they had to appeal to 16-year-olds as well, they would think about it a bit. If they don't it might not have much effect on turnout because it is just a percentage of the people who are allowed to vote.

Some people say that people who are 16 haven't got much experience of life but they know all about the problems their families face. We will know more about the system than most people because we will have studied Citizenship all the time we are at school. Older people have less idea about what is going on.

At the moment we are not represented at all. We pay our taxes and all those other things but we do not have a voice. Giving us the vote would mean that we can have our say.

I believe that people should be able to vote at 16 because all the arguments for it are much stronger than the view that we are not mature enough.

Leave margin blank

Theme 3

The global

3.1 Global business   110–127

village

What is an economy?

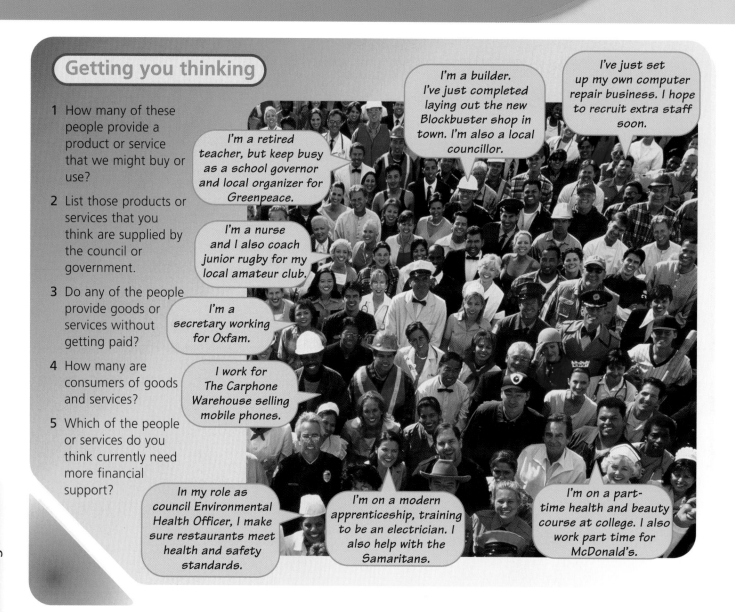

Getting you thinking

1 How many of these people provide a product or service that we might buy or use?

2 List those products or services that you think are supplied by the council or government.

3 Do any of the people provide goods or services without getting paid?

4 How many are consumers of goods and services?

5 Which of the people or services do you think currently need more financial support?

I'm a retired teacher, but keep busy as a school governor and local organizer for Greenpeace.

I'm a nurse and I also coach junior rugby for my local amateur club.

I'm a secretary working for Oxfam.

I work for The Carphone Warehouse selling mobile phones.

In my role as council Environmental Health Officer, I make sure restaurants meet health and safety standards.

I'm a builder. I've just completed laying out the new Blockbuster shop in town. I'm also a local councillor.

I've just set up my own computer repair business. I hope to recruit extra staff soon.

I'm on a modern apprenticeship, training to be an electrician. I also help with the Samaritans.

I'm on a part-time health and beauty course at college. I also work part time for McDonald's.

What is an economy?

Everyone in the United Kingdom is part of the **economy** as a consumer, producer or citizen.

We are all consumers: whatever our age, we buy the products of business.

Some of us are producers who help make products or provide services. That includes the part-time employee for McDonald's, as well as the secretary working for Oxfam.

The economy is measured by adding up either the value of everything that is produced, or the value of everything consumed, in one year. Both calculations should come to the same amount. For the UK in 2005, this figure reached over £800 billion. This works out at over £13 000 per person and about £40 000 per employee per year.

Private and public sector

Most of the things we buy are made by businesses in the **private sector**. These businesses are run by individuals or **shareholders**. A shareholder owns part of the company but leaves the organization to its managers. The main objective of businesses in the private sector is to make a **profit** for their owners, but the private sector also includes charities that raise money for good causes.

The rest of the economy is owned or run by the government and local councils. This is called the **public sector**. It includes social services, fire and police, education, defence, law, community and sports centres, housing and transport. A key objective for the public sector is to satisfy local residents. If it fails to do so, the political party that controls the council may not be re-elected at the next election.

You will find out what we mean by the economy.

The power of competition

The economy is fired by people wanting to buy things. Businesses will provide these things if there is a profit to be made. If consumers buy less of a product, less will be produced. The resources that were used to make it may be used by another business for another purpose. Food shops in town centres have closed because people use out-of-town supermarkets. The empty shops, the resources, are now used by other businesses, such as mobile phone shops. Businesses want to make a profit and will look for new opportunities.

What effect does competition have on business?

What would happen if everyone had to pay for healthcare?

Is it fair?

People who don't have enough money to pay for things they need and want aren't able to have them.

If everything was provided by the private sector, many people would suffer. If you can't afford education and are in poor health, it can be difficult to find a job and do the things other people do.

As a result, the government provides these public sector services and other social benefits. Some are free for all, whilst others are provided according to need. We pay taxes to cover the costs of these and other services.

Who does what?

Getting you thinking

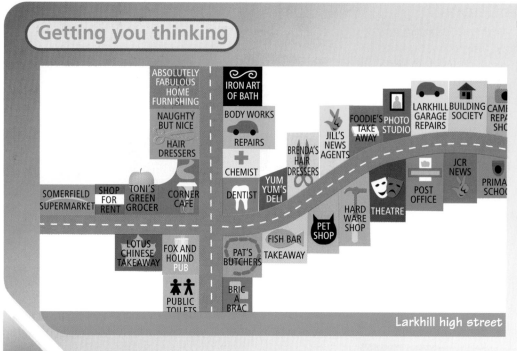

Larkhill high street

1 How many businesses are shown on the map?

2 Which businesses either support or depend on others?

3 Some businesses are similar, which means they are in competition with each other. Which businesses are these?

4 Estimate how many employees you think this high street has.

5 Which parts of the high street might the council be involved in?

6 How is Larkhill similar and different from your local high street?

Small businesses

In order to survive, businesses need to make a profit. This means their income from sales must be more than the money they spend on things such as wages, rent and buying stock. These payments out are called costs. A business makes a loss if more money is spent running it than it receives from its customers. If a business keeps making losses, it will collapse.

These businesses need each other. Jill needs suppliers to provide her shop with stock. If the suppliers fail to deliver the newspapers on time, Jill will not be able to provide what the customers want, and 'Jill's Newsagents' will lose business. Suppliers depend on newsagents because they sell their stock. The two businesses are **interdependent**.

Most of Larkhill's businesses are probably run by one person. This is fine for small businesses but bigger businesses are usually companies that are owned by many shareholders.

Interdependency

Many businesses are dependent on each other. Here are a few of the links to 'Jill's Newsagents':

- The bus company allows customers to travel to Larkhill.

- The local bank allows customers to take out loans and pay in cash from their sales.

- Suppliers of local and national newspapers, magazines and confectionery provide stock.

- The local window cleaner cleans the shop windows every week.

- Electricity suppliers provide power to all the shops and offices.

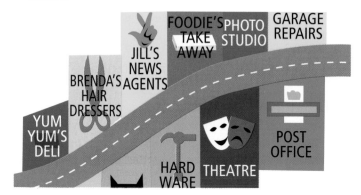

You will discover how people and resources are organized to produce goods and services, and that businesses are interdependent.

Specialization

There are many different jobs involved in making a product. The flow chart shows how a newspaper reaches the customers.

Each stage needs different types of people to do different jobs: the printers know how to print and the designer is an expert in design. The distributors need drivers and the newsagents have close contact with their customers who want to buy the paper. All the people and businesses involved are **specialized** in the type of work they do.

Journalists, photographers, editors, advertising staff, designers, etc., to lay out newspapers

Printers to produce the newspaper or magazine

Newsagents

Transport to distribute product to newsagents

Division of labour

If one person did all the jobs needed to sell newspapers, they would have to write the articles, design the pages, print the paper, take it to a shop and sell it. The newspaper would take far too long to produce and it would be of low quality. It's much quicker and more efficient in costs and quality if each stage is carried out by people who are expert in their field. This is known as **division of labour**. It works in many parts of the economy and means that the country produces more and makes us better off.

Action

1 Choose a small shopping area or industrial estate near you and make a simple map of the businesses there.
2 Show how one of the businesses uses division of labour and/or specialization to be more efficient.

Check your understanding

1 Choose a small business in your local area and list as many of its links as you can.
2 Why do you think you have specialist teachers in your secondary school, but a class teacher in your primary school?
3 What different types of non-teaching jobs are there in your school?
4 Why would your school be less well run if your teachers had to carry out all the tasks currently done by non-teachers?
5 How does the division of labour work in a restaurant? How does it help the business to be more efficient?

What's your opinion?

'People would be happier if they were responsible for making the whole product rather than just part of it.'
Do you agree with this statement? Give reasons for your opinion, showing you have considered another point of view.

Key Terms

division of labour: where employees concentrate on a particular task or job at which they are expert

interdependent: where businesses need each other to survive

specialized: where employees or businesses concentrate on tasks that they can do well

Sharing success or failure

Getting you thinking

The Carphone Warehouse started trading in 1989. It now has over 1085 stores in 12 countries, and employs over 12 000 people. Its sales income is over £2.35 billion. The Carphone Warehouse also actively supports charity work. It helps Get Connected, a helpline for children and young people under 25 who are, for whatever reason, vulnerable to danger. The charity's HQ is based at the company's offices.

'I would have been amazed to be told that, within 15 months of joining the company, I would be managing a superstore.'

Julie Checkley,
Area Sales Manager

'We pride ourselves in giving our customers simple, impartial advice.'

1 In what ways can the business claim to be successful?

2 How might The Carphone Warehouse be contributing to the economy?

3 What evidence is there to suggest that The Carphone Warehouse could be a good employer?

4 What evidence is there that The Carphone Warehouse helps the community?

Going for growth

At The Carphone Warehouse, success comes from the growing market for mobile phones and providing good customer service. The mobile phone business is very competitive so The Carphone Warehouse has to invest in new buildings and equipment so that they keep ahead of competitors. It also needs to employ, train and motivate the staff.

Supporting individuals

Businesses can support the individuals who work for them. Employees receive incomes and training to develop their skills. Many of these skills are transferable. Individuals will be able to use, or transfer, skills such as good customer service to a new job.

Supporting communities

Employees will help local businesses by spending some of their income in local shops, pubs, cafés and restaurants.

Businesses pay taxes from their profits and people pay taxes from their earnings. They also pay tax when they buy things. These taxes provide the government and local councils with money that can be used to benefit the community.

Supporting the wider community

A growing business helps to create or support jobs in other, interdependent, businesses. These jobs may be in the local community, but others might be further away. A growing business will do things like:

- communicate more
- use more energy and water
- buy extra equipment such as computers
- buy more materials from suppliers
- buy more services from other businesses.

All these contributions help the country's economy to grow. Successful businesses often create jobs and pay more taxes, so people benefit.

You will understand the consequences of success and failure of businesses on individuals, communities and beyond.

Markets moving on

The market for UK coal moved on. That is to say, it changed. Two reasons for this are:

- oil and gas are often cheaper and cleaner alternatives
- coal from other countries is cheaper.

When markets move on, people may lose their jobs. Some of the businesses that supported the declining industry will either close down or look for new markets in an attempt to survive. Local shops and traders will lose out because people have less money to spend.

Those employees made redundant may have the wrong skills for new types of businesses. New businesses are unlikely to start up in areas where people don't have the skills they need, or where other businesses are failing.

Markets failing communities

The market system is said to have failed a community when unemployment is much higher than in other parts of the country.

3.1: Global business

Action

Find out about:

- a business in your area that helps the community
- businesses that have closed down: can you work out why?
- new businesses that have moved in: can you work out why?

Check your understanding

1 How can an employee benefit from working for a business?
2 How might growing businesses create jobs both in the local community and beyond?
3 In what other ways can businesses help the community?
4 How do businesses and their employees provide money for local services?
5 What knock-on effects might there be when a big employer in a local community closes down?
6 How might the government reduce the impact of a big employer closing down?
7 What would happen if more businesses were closing down than expanding in the country?

What's your opinion?

'Businesses just want to make a profit.'
Do you agree with this statement? Give reasons for your opinion, showing you have considered another point of view.

Economic decline and growth

It is natural for some businesses to grow and others to decline. The market system brings about a shift of resources towards making things that are most in demand. The economy will grow if the value of the new sales of the expanding businesses is greater than the value lost from declining businesses. If it is the other way round, however, the economy is declining.

Where this happens, the government needs to step in to help. By introducing **retraining** schemes, and investing in roads and other communications, it can make areas where lots of people are unemployed more attractive to new businesses.

Key Terms

retraining: learning new skills that can be used in a different job

When prices rise

Getting you thinking

The changing value of money

£1000 in 1971 would buy as much as £8612 in 2005

£1000 in 1981 would buy as much as £2337 in 2005

£1000 in 1991 would buy as much as £1309 in 2005

1 What happens to the value of money over time?

2 If a small car cost £1000 in 1971, what might you expect to pay for it today?

3 What do people expect to happen to their pay?

What does this type of car cost today?

How does inflation happen?

Inflation happens when things we buy get more expensive as time passes. It often comes about because people want to spend more. In fact it's one big circle:

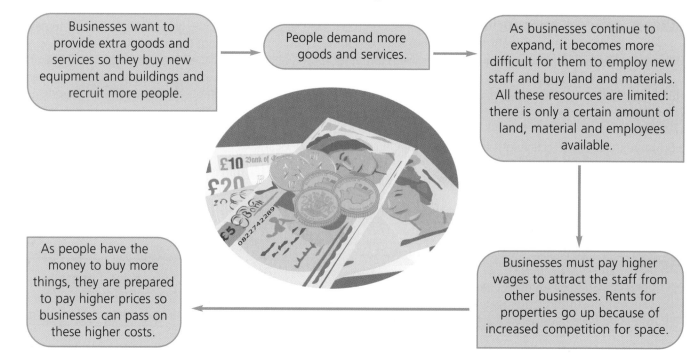

Businesses want to provide extra goods and services so they buy new equipment and buildings and recruit more people.

→

People demand more goods and services.

→

As businesses continue to expand, it becomes more difficult for them to employ new staff and buy land and materials. All these resources are limited: there is only a certain amount of land, material and employees available.

↓

Businesses must pay higher wages to attract the staff from other businesses. Rents for properties go up because of increased competition for space.

←

As people have the money to buy more things, they are prepared to pay higher prices so businesses can pass on these higher costs.

You will find out what causes inflation, the problems of inflation and how it might be controlled.

Who is affected by rising prices?

People who save will lose out: the value of their savings will not buy so much in the future.

People with incomes that do not grow at the **rate of inflation** will also lose out. This will include pensions that are not linked to the inflation rate.

UK businesses can also lose out if inflation in other countries is at a lower rate. The price rises make our products and services more expensive to buy. Borrowers will gain because the value of their debt will fall.

Can it go too far?

A little bit of inflation (about 2% each year) doesn't do any harm. However, if prices rise too fast, businesses start losing money because people stop buying their products. To stay in business, companies cut their costs by making people redundant. This may keep the business going, but unemployment will rise.

If pensions don't increase at the same rate as inflation, pensioners can suffer

What can be done to control inflation?

There are three ways in which inflation can be controlled:

- **Change interest rates**

    Every month, the Bank of England decides whether to change interest rates or keep them the same. If the Bank believes inflation will increase, it raises interest rates. The cost of borrowing will increase so people will buy less.

- **Make sure there are enough staff**

    A shortage of trained people makes wages go up. One way of reducing inflation is to make sure that there are plenty of people with the right skills. The government can provide training courses and help businesses train their staff.

- **Keep business costs down**

    In order to remain competitive, businesses will try to reduce their costs. They need to reduce their costs by keeping their payments for materials, land and staff as low as possible. They may need to reorganize so they are making their products as efficiently as possible. They will want to keep prices down to attract consumers.

3.1: Global business

Action

What is the UK's current rate of inflation? Is this seen as good for the country? You could look at www.treasury.gov.uk.

Check your understanding

1 In your own words, explain what inflation is.
2 Name two things that can cause inflation. Explain why these things can lead to an increase in prices.
3 How might inflation affect someone who:
   a) is saving money?
   b) has a pension that is not linked to inflation?
   c) has trained in an area of work where there is a skills shortage, such as computer programming?
   d) is working in a business that is losing money and who doesn't have any specialist skills?
4 What can businesses do to help keep inflation rates down?

What's your opinion?

'Inflation creates more winners than losers.'
Do you agree with this statement? Give reasons for your opinion, showing you have considered another point of view.

Key Terms

economic growth: this happens when the country produces more goods and services from year to year
inflation: the general rise in prices
rate of inflation: the rate at which prices rise

Making ends meet

Getting you thinking

Borrowing

> We took out a £120 000 mortgage. This is twice my partner's and my joint salaries. Our daughter has taken out a student loan to go to university. I took out a loan to buy a new car. This summer we went to Florida using our credit cards.

> I own four properties and rent the rooms to students. The rent, after taking away costs, gives me an income of £47 000 over the year. I also own shares in several companies and I earned £3000 from them this year. I earn £50 000 a year from my job. I'm going to take out another mortgage and buy another property.

1 What is the income of each person?

2 What do you understand by the term 'borrowing'?

3 Rank the people according to who you think earns the most to the least.

4 Who is finding it most difficult to sort out their finances, and why?

> My work is looking after my three children and making ends meet. I'm a single parent. The £100 I get from benefits doesn't cover my food and bills. I'm already behind in my rent and have had to borrow from the local moneylender. If I don't pay it back, he will take my furniture. I've had to take on evening cleaning work, earning £30 a week, with my sister baby-sitting my children.

Spending or saving?

People use the money they earn each month to buy products and services. If, once they have spent money on what they need, there is some of their monthly income left, they can put the remainder into savings.

If they need to spend more than they earn and haven't enough income to cover their outgoings, they may decide to borrow money or use their savings.

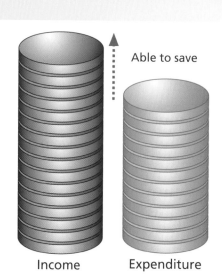

Able to save

Income   Expenditure

Has to use past savings or borrow money

Income   Expenditure

You will find out why borrowing money can cause problems and how people can be protected from poverty.

Is borrowing the solution?

If you want to borrow money, you must find someone to lend it. You will pay **interest** on the loan. This is an amount of money paid in addition to the amount borrowed. It is only safe to borrow money if you know you can pay it back.

People with low incomes and low skills will find it hard to borrow because it will be difficult for them to repay the loan. They may be below the **poverty line** and at risk of being economically excluded from society. This means that they don't have enough money to pay for the goods and services they need, such as housing, food and heating. Children in these situations can never have a birthday party or go to the cinema, so they really feel left out.

In Britain, 17% of the population is living below the poverty line, and in more than one in six families, nobody works. The poorest 20% earn 8% of all earnings, compared with the 42% earned by the top 20% of earners.

Fairer shares

The government uses some of the money it raises from taxes to help the poor. It provides benefits, free healthcare and education for all and subsidized housing. People who earn more pay more taxes. Poorer people receive more help. This is called **redistributing income**.

Providing real opportunities

The government doesn't want people to depend on benefits all the time. It wants them to be able to support themselves and become an active part of the economy. The government trains people in different skills and encourages them to seek work.

Minimum wage

£200m of government money and £100m lottery money pays for neighbourhood nursery places so parents can work.

More retraining opportunities

Working family tax credit means low earners can keep more of their income after tax.

1 Why would a government want to spend money on the schemes shown in the newspaper headlines? How could these schemes help?

2 Which schemes increase skills and which increase the rewards for working?

Action

Discussion point: Do you think it could be a problem for the whole of society if some people are economically excluded?

Check your understanding

1 Why do people borrow?
2 What does being economically excluded from society mean?
3 The government receives money from taxes. How does it use it to help the poor?
4 Why does the government run schemes to retrain people in new skills?

What's your opinion?

'Redistributing income is so unfair. I work hard for my money: why should I help pay for people who don't work?'

Do you agree with this statement? Give reasons for your opinion, showing you have considered another point of view.

Key Terms

interest: extra payment paid to a lender by someone who has borrowed some money

poverty line: the income level below which someone cannot afford to live

redistributing income: taking money from wealthier people through taxation, to give it to poorer people through benefits

Can the world be fairer?

Getting you thinking

1 What evidence is there to suggest that the UK is better off than Niger?

2 What data might suggest the gap between the two countries is increasing?

3 Do you think the cost of buying basic needs is the same?

Compare some facts about Niger and the UK

	Niger	UK
How much the economy is worth per citizen	$190	$26,4440
How fast the economy grew	−0·8% decline of $15 per person	2·4% increase of $635 per person
Doctors per 1000 people	3	164
How long people live	46 years	78 years
Number of children dying before the age of 5 for every 1000 people	265	7
Internet users per 1000 people	1·3	423·1
Adults who can read	17%	100%
International aid	Receives aid	Gives aid
Free education, healthcare and state pensions	No	Yes

Source: Human Development Report 2005

LEDCs and MEDCs

The world falls into two groups:

- The more economically developed countries (**MEDCs**), like the UK
- The less economically developed countries (**LEDCs**), like Niger and The Gambia.

This is a crude way of splitting the world into rich and poor countries. It masks different rates of economic growth and some countries do not fit into one group or another.

People living in Niger.
How does their standard of living compare with yours?

Debt: a cause of poverty?

41 poor countries, 33 of them in Africa, owe about £150 billion in foreign debt. Every day, the poorest countries of Sub-Saharan Africa pay £20 million of their debt to the West, whilst their economies decline, infant mortality rises and life expectancy falls.

To repay these debts, poor countries are forced to divert money away from healthcare, education and other vital services. Many children don't get the chance to go to school, mothers don't have prenatal care, and HIV-infected persons don't get the treatment they need.

The beginnings of international debt

In the 1970s, the world's richest nations lent huge sums of money to poorer countries. This money was sometimes lent to undemocratic, corrupt governments. Much of it was spent on weapons, or wasted. It wasn't used to develop the country or help people living in poverty.

Many indebted countries, like Niger, are unable to escape the poverty trap because their economies have been growing at a slower rate than that of other countries. They are often dependent on selling one or two primary products, such as oil, bananas, uranium, copper or coffee. The prices they get for these products have fallen. This means they need to borrow more to maintain the same level of imports. This causes greater debt.

You will discover why it is so difficult for some poor countries to develop.

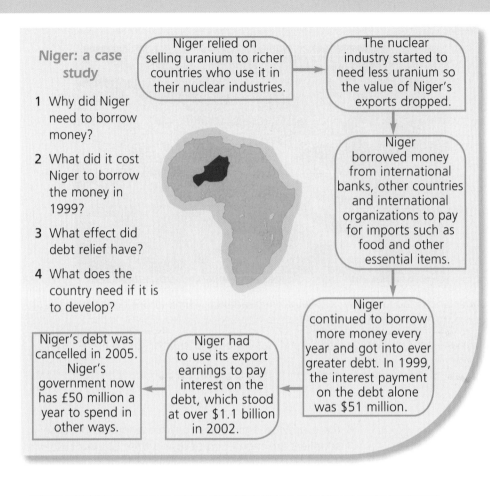

Niger: a case study

1 Why did Niger need to borrow money?

2 What did it cost Niger to borrow the money in 1999?

3 What effect did debt relief have?

4 What does the country need if it is to develop?

Niger relied on selling uranium to richer countries who use it in their nuclear industries.

The nuclear industry started to need less uranium so the value of Niger's exports dropped.

Niger borrowed money from international banks, other countries and international organizations to pay for imports such as food and other essential items.

Niger continued to borrow more money every year and got into ever greater debt. In 1999, the interest payment on the debt alone was $51 million.

Niger had to use its export earnings to pay interest on the debt, which stood at over $1.1 billion in 2002.

Niger's debt was cancelled in 2005. Niger's government now has £50 million a year to spend in other ways.

Cancelling the debt

Some debts have already been cancelled and there is a programme for future debt cancellations. This has made a difference. In Uganda, twice as many children are now attending primary school. In Mozambique, they can now afford to vaccinate children against whooping cough, tetanus and diphtheria.

World leaders have promised to halve the amount of global poverty by 2015. But Kofi Annan, Secretary General of the United Nations, says "Without debt cancellation, this target is a pipe dream."

Action

What is happening to world debt? Look up: www.oneworld.net, www.oxfam.org, www.dfid.gov.uk, and www.worldbank.org (and go to the schools section).

Check your understanding

1 What are LEDCs and MEDCs?
2 Why can't indebted countries spend much money on vital services like health and education?
3 How did some governments damage their country's chances?
4 Give two reasons why it is difficult for the economies of LEDCs to grow.
5 Why would indebted countries be in a better situation if their debts were cancelled?

What's your opinion?

'Debt should only be cancelled in countries where people's human rights are respected.'
Do you agree with this statement? Give reasons for your opinion, showing you have considered another point of view.

Key Terms

LEDC: a less economically developed country

MEDC: a more economically developed country

Globalization

Getting you thinking

In an average week, you will eat food from a dozen different countries, and in this way, you will be linked to people all over the world. We depend on them to grow food; they depend on us to buy it.

1 List some advantages and disadvantages of this interdependence. Think about economic, social and environmental issues.

2 Do you think this interdependence means the world has become a 'smaller' place?

A shrinking world

Modern technology, combined with improved communication and transportation, has made it easier to trade around the world. Our nations are interdependent. It is not really the countries themselves that trade, but the businesses and consumers within those countries. The importance of trade is likely to increase with advances in technology. Already the Internet allows us to buy from anywhere in the world.

Added together, local economies, right down to the smallest local high streets, help make up a nation's economy. Added together, national economies make up the world economy.

The globalization game

Globalization has many players. Consumers, employees, large companies and nations all take part. There are winners and losers.

Consumer power:
Consumers have power because they can buy from someone else if they don't like the price or quality. Businesses often try to produce as cheaply as possible in order to attract customers. People can choose whether to pay the lowest prices or spend a bit more and buy things that have been produced more fairly.

Producer power:
Producers have power because many businesses are very large. They can:

- force down the price they pay for resources because suppliers are frightened of losing their biggest customer
- keep wages down, because workers have few alternative jobs to go to
- fix prices higher if there is no competition
- fail to look after the environment if there are no laws to protect it.

Who is more powerful: big businesses or nations?

Economy of Republic of Ireland	$122 billion
Microsoft's sales	$36·8 billion
Economy of Niger	$2·2 billion

Source: Human Development Report 2005; www.microsoft.com

Some companies' sales are bigger than many countries' economies. A country is stuck in one place (it can't move), whereas a multinational company can produce wherever costs are lowest. Products, such as trainers, are often made in countries where labour is cheap. Businesses buy services from accounting to IT, from countries around the world where labour is cheap. Many countries, however, welcome multinational businesses because they provide employment and skills. This helps the economy to grow.

You will find out about the impact of globalization.

Global branding

Some people are worried that global brands such as McDonald's, Coca Cola, Pepsi, Nike and Gap erode the traditional culture of communities.

3.1: Global business

Action

Visit the Accessorize website at www.accessorize.co.uk/fairtrade.htm and find out about its trading code.

Look up a newspaper page on the Internet and search for articles about Nike, Coca Cola or McDonald's. Then visit the company's website. Try also to find websites which publish views against the company. Present your findings to the class.

Check your understanding

1 In what ways might people think that producers have too much power?
2 In what situation might a supplier agree to sell goods to a buyer for a lower price?
3 If there is high unemployment in an area, why can companies pay lower wages?
4 Why do multinational companies produce their goods and services in different countries?
5 Explain why people might be worried about global brands.

What's your opinion?

'Global companies should not be allowed to employ people in LEDCs. Do you agree with this statement? Give reasons for your opinion, showing you have considered another point of view.

Can business be good?

More and more businesses are looking closely at their impact on the communities they serve. The Body Shop, The Co-op Bank and Fairtrade organizations monitor their actions. Businesses are very aware of the damage that bad publicity can do. They run schemes to monitor their activities around the world. It is often difficult to carry this out and meet the standards set. One supplier to a high street fashion shop has 5000 home workers. The company tries to monitor what's going on, but it's hard to be perfect.

Key Terms

globalization: the increasing interdependence of the world

Sweet shops and sweatshops

Getting you thinking

Comic Relief helped a group of small farmers in Ghana, West Africa, to set up a company to trade their cocoa beans. As shareholders in the company, the farmers have a say in how their chocolate is produced and sold, and get a fair share of the profits. The farmers also ensure that employees who pick the beans are paid a fair wage.

A US government investigation found that children as young as 11 were being sold into slavery to harvest cocoa beans on the Ivory Coast. The US government wants chocolate manufacturers in the USA to label chocolate as 'Slave Free' if it has been made from cocoa from farms which do not exploit workers. The chocolate manufactures are trying to stop the government introducing this new law.

The average UK consumer spends about £60 a year on chocolate. The total world market is worth £3.8 billion a year.

1 Why did Comic Relief give money to the Ghanaian farmers?

2 Suggest one reason why the US chocolate manufacturers oppose the 'Slave Free' law.

3 Do you think the law will help the enslaved children on the Ivory Coast? Give reasons.

Making trade fairer

Trade is a very important way for any country to earn money and create jobs. People and countries have traded for thousands of years, but in today's global economy, information, goods and money can be moved around the world at an incredible speed. Companies aim to make the best product at the cheapest price.

The World Trade Organization (WTO) is responsible for negotiating international trade agreements. Most rich countries want a **free trade** system in which the prices of goods are determined by the amount that people want to buy and sell. But many people believe such a system favours richer countries like USA and Japan and want the WTO to be reformed. They argue that world trade must be managed so the poorest countries benefit more. In other words, they want world trade to become **'fair trade'**.

Fair trade is trade that is good for the producer; a system that ensures more of the price consumers pay goes to the producer. Fair trade staff would be paid a fair wage, have good working conditions and be allowed to form trade unions to defend their rights.

Fair trade campaigns, such as the Clean Clothes Campaign (CCC), have drawn attention to the working conditions of workers all around the world.

Is this farmer being paid a fair price?

You will discover how inequalities resulting from free trade can be reduced.

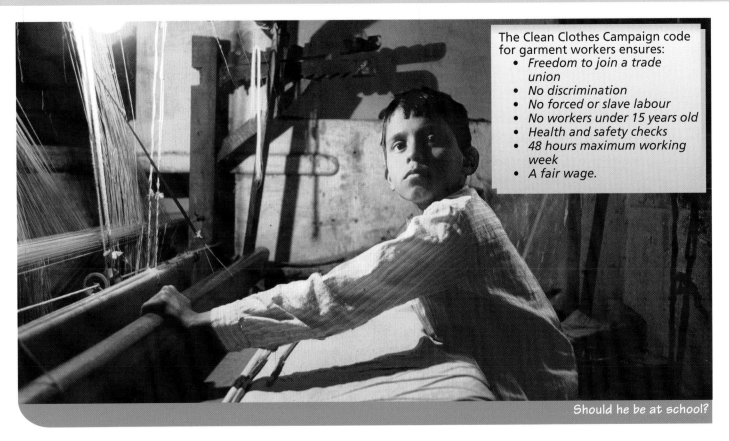

The Clean Clothes Campaign code for garment workers ensures:
- *Freedom to join a trade union*
- *No discrimination*
- *No forced or slave labour*
- *No workers under 15 years old*
- *Health and safety checks*
- *48 hours maximum working week*
- *A fair wage.*

Should he be at school?

To buy or not to buy

The Clean Clothes Campaign does not believe consumers should **boycott** goods that are not 'clean' because it believes boycotts will put employees out of work. When the US government talked about bringing in a law to stop anything made by children under 15 from being imported in the USA, many child employees in Bangladesh were thrown out of work and their families often went hungry as a result.

Action
1 Use the Internet to research UK companies trying to promote fair trade.
2 Obtain details of company 'codes' like the CCC code above. Use these to write an article on fair trade and its aims for helping workers in LEDCs.

Check your understanding
1 In your own words, say what the World Trade Organization (WTO) does.
2 Why do some people want to reform the WTO?
3 How would 'fair trade' help workers in LEDCs?
4 What human rights do groups, such as the Clean Clothes Campaign, help to protect?

What's your opinion?
'People in the UK should boycott companies that sell "dirty" clothes and trainers.'
Do you agree with this statement? Give reasons for your opinion, showing you have considered another point of view.

Key Terms
boycott: to refuse to use or have anything to do with something

fair trade: a way of buying and selling products that aims to pay the producer a fair price

free trade: trade between countries which is not restricted by things like high taxes on imports

Worth a protest?

"Free trade is like putting the rabbit and the tiger in the same cage, the rabbit being the poor countries," claims a protestor.

Think of some reasons why people might agree or disagree with this statement.

The unacceptable face of protest

Protest

Anti-globalization protests are a regular feature on the news. The protests are greatest when international organizations such as the International Monetary Fund (IMF) and World Trade Organization (WTO) meet to discuss free trade, poverty and wealth. The protestors are drawn from various pressure groups. This increases the number of protestors, but means their protests lack a clear aim. Some protestors are concerned with global warming, others with poverty, and still others worry about the impact of multinationals.

One such pressure group is the WDM (World Development Movement), which wants to change world trade rules. It is calling for strong international rules that put people's needs before free trade. It claims that money needed for clean water, health and education in poor countries is still being handed over to rich countries in debt repayments.

Receiving the right message

Your own views on an issue will be determined by what you hear. For some this will come from discussions with like-minded people. For most, the source will be the TV news or from their favourite newspaper.

Whichever way, there is a danger that the information is biased. Biased information will favour one side or another, so it is always useful to hear both sides of the argument.

When the issue is global it can be more difficult to get your opinion across, because you have to influence powerful nations or world institutions. Again, pressure groups have a role to play in influencing opinion and providing an alternative view.

The work of international organizations

Three major international trade organizations are:

- The World Trade Organization, which helps shape rules about trade so that it makes selling to other countries easier.

- The World Bank, which provides loans to poorer countries for projects to help reduce poverty.

- The International Monetary Fund, which promotes international financial cooperation and economic growth of international trade.

You will find out about the arguments behind anti-globalization protests.

Who says what?

The anti-globalization movement says:	The international trade organizations say:
• International organizations, such as the IMF and World Bank, cause poverty because they encourage free trade. This can damage LEDCs because they have to compete in world markets. • The movement itself represents the poor, who have no voice themselves.	• Globalization and free trade is good for the poor. More international trade brings more jobs to poorer countries. Therefore it brings greater prosperity to the world and reduces poverty. • Protest groups are undemocratic because they haven't been elected and so they cannot claim to represent people. • Protest groups are, in effect, preventing global efforts to tackle poverty.

How can pressure groups make their voices heard?

Pressure groups can lobby governments throughout the world and try to persuade them to their point of view. The groups can promote their case through publicity, including their Internet sites, and they can protest in other ways.

Some recent protests have involved outbreaks of violence and damage to buildings. McDonald's is seen as a symbol of multinationals and is an easy target. Such actions by protestors, however few, are breaking the law. It gets media attention, but the protesters may lose the sympathy of the public.

Action

Look at the following websites for more information about globalization and prepare a short report on the arguments for and against increased globalization.

www.oneworld.net   www.worldbank.org

www.wto.org   www.oxfam.org.uk

www.dfid.gov.uk   www.imf.org

Check your understanding

1 Why have different pressure groups joined together at certain world trade demonstrations? Make a list of the advantages and disadvantages of them doing so.

2 What other methods might pressure groups use to get their message across?

3 Why might pressure groups show bias when putting their case across?

4 Might businesses and governments show bias too?

What's your opinion?

'The European Union has much higher import taxes on chocolate than cocoa beans. It should continue to do so.'

Do you agree with this statement? Give reasons for your opinion, showing you have considered another point of view.

What is sustainable development?

Theme 3: The global village

Getting you thinking

Imagine you live in a very poor country, in a small rural village. You need fuel to cook food for your family. You may also need fuel to boil your drinking water to stop your children getting sick. The only way to get this fuel is to cut down the trees near your village. But you know that if you do this, the precious topsoil will blow away and eventually the desert will swallow up your village.

1 What might happen if you don't boil your drinking water?

2 What are the long-term consequences if you cut down the trees for fuel?

3 Suggest possible solutions to this problem.

Hard choices

The villagers have to make the hard choice between solving a problem they have now and not making problems for the future. This kind of choice has to be made by everybody, although the circumstances are different everywhere.

In the UK and other MEDCs where there is economic growth, people expect their standard of living to improve. People can buy all sorts of things to make life more comfortable. They usually work shorter hours and have better access to healthcare and education.

These can all be good things but there are some drawbacks.

Growing food and building homes, roads, schools and hospitals uses land, energy and resources. The demand for products and services can mean pollution increases and natural resources are used up. In time, these factors could actually decrease the standard of living. So the choice is between having what we want now or making sure future generations don't suffer.

1 List some of the land, energy and resources used in the following:

- growing food
- building motorways
- foreign holidays.

Sustainable development

Sustainable development means we can improve the way people live today, without harming the prospects for the future. Different resources can be used so that scarce or dangerous materials are no longer needed. New materials can be designed to use less energy. Standards of living can be improved in ways that protect the environment, and harmful products can stop being made.

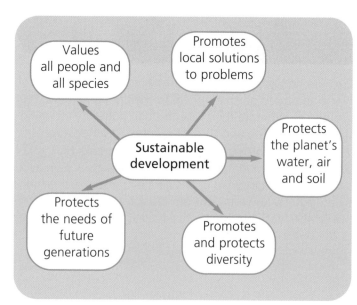

You will find out about sustainable development and consider ways in which it can be achieved.

Sustainable solutions

Energy

As supplies of coal, oil and natural gas are limited, they will only sustain our needs for so long before we will be forced to find alternative, sustainable sources of energy.

One solution could be wind power. The UK already has many wind farms, mostly in Wales, Scotland and Cornwall. The amount of electricity generated by wind power in Europe rose by 20% in 2004. Offshore wind farms could, in theory, produce twice the UK's electricity requirements.

Food

For decades, large UK and European fishing fleets have fished in the North Sea. In recent years it became clear that fish stocks there were so low that there was a real danger the North Sea would be fished out. Over-fishing had not allowed enough time for fish to breed and stocks to recover. Now fishing here is strictly controlled. Stocks are starting to recover and are a sustainable resource for the future.

Resources

Similarly, if you cut down forests for timber and paper faster than nature can replace them, you will end up with no trees.

However, trees are a **renewable** resource. Many countries now plant fast-growing trees to replace those chopped down. You now often see goods labelled: 'Made from timber from a sustainable forest'.

A sustainable solution

Village Aid is a UK charity that works with people in the poorest regions of West Africa. All their projects aim to promote sustainable development. This is one such project.

Every day, women from Janneh Kunda, a village in The Gambia, must walk from their homes to the rice fields. In the rainy season this can be dangerous. The bridges are old, unsafe and slippery with mud. The women have to carry tools, food for the day and their children. They must also carry the rice back home. The local people discussed these problems and decided they needed a safe bridge. It was built using the back end of an old lorry (which had been left for scrap), other local materials and local labour. It cost around £2000, a tiny sum of money by western standards, and will last 25 years.

1 Can the Janneh Kunda bridge be described as a sustainable solution to the women's problem? Give reasons.

Action

Organizations such as Comic Relief, Oxfam, Christian Aid, Action Aid and many more sponsor sustainable development projects. Research the work of one or more of these organizations and identify two to three problems they have addressed, and the solutions they and their local partners employed.

Check your understanding

1 In your own words, explain what is meant by 'sustainable development'.
2 Give one reason why it will be important in future to find sustainable solutions to environmental problems.
3 Why are the following considered to be sustainable developments?
    • digging wells • building schools • planting trees
4 Can wind power be described as a sustainable energy source? Give reasons.
5 Why has commercial fishing in the North Sea been restricted?

What's your opinion?

'We should pay higher taxes on energy from non-sustainable sources.' Do you agree with this statement? Give reasons for your opinion, showing you have considered another point of view.

Key Terms

renewable: able to be replaced or restored

sustainable development: living now in a way that doesn't damage the needs of future generations

Local solutions to global problems

Researchers from Sheffield University asked 2000 nine-to sixteen-year-olds from all around the country what they thought about their town centres. Most, but not all, described their home towns in negative terms.

The young people surveyed said they wanted more police, more security cameras and spaces where they could meet, where they would be safe and not be considered 'a nuisance' by adults.

1 Why did the young people want more security cameras?

2 "Kids today don't care about their neighbourhood. They mess everything up with graffiti and litter." Do you agree or disagree? Give reasons.

3 If you could talk to the architects who plan city centres, what improvements would you suggest?

Is Agenda 21 the answer?

At the United Nation's 'Earth Summit' in Rio de Janeiro in 1992, member countries agreed to work together to promote sustainable development around the world. **Local Agenda 21** (LA21) sets out how this is to be done at a local level. Although LA21 is a 'global' plan, it stresses the importance of involving local people when planning projects. They should be asked what they want for their local area. Local people often have valuable knowledge and experience, and are more likely to support a project if they feel they 'own' it. All LA21 projects should provide for the needs of the local community as a whole, and not exclude or discriminate against any group or minority.

Since 1992, local councils in the UK have been working with local people on a wide range of projects. These are some of the long-term aims of the LA21 projects.

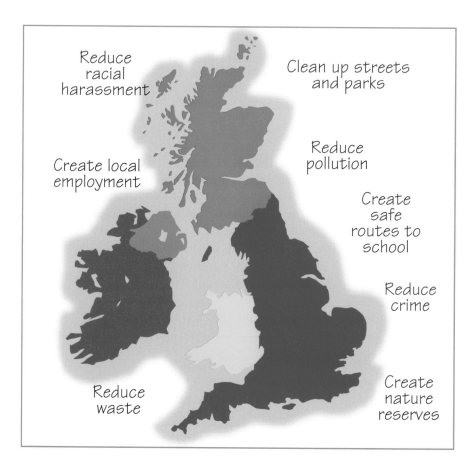

Reduce racial harassment

Clean up streets and parks

Create local employment

Reduce pollution

Create safe routes to school

Reduce crime

Reduce waste

Create nature reserves

You will find out about Local Agenda 21.

LA21 in action: at home and abroad

Oldham, Lancashire

How people in Oldham think their community can be improved:

- Tackle street crime
- Improve street lighting
- More police on the beat
- More drugs education
- Improve health services
- Make people more aware of links between health and environment.

When the people of Oldham were asked about health as part of their LA21 plans, they didn't just comment on local hospitals and doctors. They also mentioned a wide range of social problems, including crime and violence, noisy and aggressive neighbours, drug abuse and pollution. Good health isn't just an absence of disease, they argued. Stress-related illness can be just as serious as physical illness such as heart disease.

Oxford

A local primary school uses a 'walking bus' to reduce car journeys to and from school. The walking bus, like an ordinary bus, has stops where parents wait to drop off and pick up their children, and a regular route and timetable. However, rather than use a motorized bus, everyone walks. Twenty to twenty-five children use the 'bus' every day.

Chicago, USA

Rooftop gardens in the heart of Chicago will improve the air quality in the city because the plants absorb carbon dioxide and produce oxygen. The gardens will keep the sun's heat off the buildings, making them cooler and cut down the energy needed for air conditioning. The gardens also encourage birds to nest in the heart of the city.

Vaxjo, Sweden

Local people have voted to phase out the use of fossil fuels in all council buildings and transport. All new council buildings will be fitted with solar energy panels, and city buses will run on methane gas.

Action

Find out if your local council is promoting LA21 projects. For example, are they trying to reduce traffic congestion, pollution and noise? Are they introducing traffic calming schemes or trying to make streets safer for children and older residents?

Check your understanding

1 In your own words, what is the main aim of Local Agenda 21?
2 Which of the LA21 aims do you think is the most important for your local area? Give reasons.
3 Pick two of the four LA21 projects above and say if they offer sustainable solutions. Give reasons.

What's your opinion?

'Local solutions are likely to be more successful than global solutions.' Do you agree with this statement? Give reasons for your opinion, showing you have considered another point of view.

Key Terms

Local Agenda 21: a global plan to ask local people how they think their immediate environment could be improved

Waste not, want not

"That polystyrene coffee cup you got from the vending machine, and are just about to bin, could be turned into a pencil. Thousands of acres of forest are felled every year to make pencils, but that doesn't have to happen," says inventor Edward Douglas-Miller of Remarkable Pencils, which produces 20 000 recycled plastic pens and pencils a day.
www.remarkable.co.uk

Cash from trash

In Liverpool, CREATE employs people who are long-term unemployed to fix old electrical equipment for resale. They get paid and work towards an NVQ in engineering assembly. Many former trainees have found permanent jobs elsewhere.

Xerox are now selling photocopiers with 'remanufactured' parts. The company takes back its own end-of-life photocopiers, and builds new machines out of reconditioned parts that are still in good condition. Reused and recycled parts can comprise up to 90% of a remanufactured machine's weight. Xerox estimates that it saves US$200 million each year on purchases of new materials. The company designs its products with a 'waste-free' goal, aiming for all components to be reusable or recyclable.

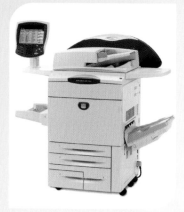

1 In what ways can the three projects in action below be described as 'environmentally friendly'?

2 Why do you think these projects were started?

3 Are these projects sustainable? Give reasons.

Getting rid of waste

Each person in the European Union produces 1 kg of household waste per day; which means a family of four produces 1 500 kg (more than the weight of a 5-door saloon car) every year.

EU household waste disposal

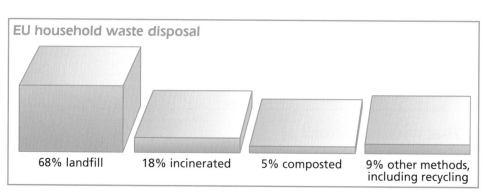

68% landfill   18% incinerated   5% composted   9% other methods, including recycling

Source: www.europa.eu.int

You will discover how waste disposal causes local environmental problems and consider some sustainable solutions.

Dump it?

Throwing rubbish into large holes is convenient, but there are problems with this. Modern materials such as plastics do not rot and others can pollute the soil or groundwater. **Biodegradable** material, such as kitchen and garden waste, produces methane gas (a **greenhouse gas**) when it decays (see page 136).

In 1995, all EU countries agreed to reduce the amount of biodegradable rubbish in landfill sites and set the targets in the graph on the right.

Burn it?

The UK government plans to incinerate more rubbish, but there are concerns about airborne pollution from incinerators. The latest incinerators are less polluting and more energy efficient than earlier types. But environmental groups opposed to incineration, such as Friends of the Earth, claim they still produce significant levels of dangerous chemicals, including dioxins. Many medical experts think there are links between dioxins and cancer. They believe that dioxins can affect children's growth, and even low levels are known to affect people's immune systems.

Recycle it?

There is some disagreement over how much waste can realistically be recycled. Friends of the Earth argue that 80% of all household waste could be recycled or composted. Germany, Netherlands and Switzerland already **recycle** 50% of household waste, compared to the UK's 16%.

The aim in the UK is to push recycling levels up to 60%. From an economic point of view, recycling is only viable if it costs less than using new materials, or if people want to pay the difference.

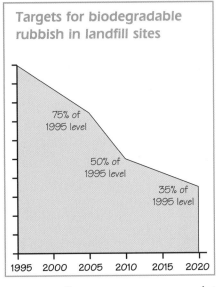

Targets for biodegradable rubbish in landfill sites

Source: www.europa.eu.int

Action

1 How could household waste be minimized? How could shops help with this problem?
2 How is household waste disposed of in your area? What plans does your council have to reduce the amount of biodegradable material it puts into landfill sites?
3 If everyone composted their biodegradable waste, would this have a significant effect on how much rubbish would have to go into landfill sites? Give a reason.
4 Is recycling the only safe solution to waste disposal?

Check your understanding

1 Describe the advantages and disadvantages associated with using:
   a) landfill sites and b) incinerators.
2 Are landfill sites 'sustainable'? Give reasons.

What's your opinion?

'Households should be fined if they don't recycle their waste.'
Do you agree with this statement? Give reasons for your opinion, showing you have considered another point of view.

Key Terms

biodegradable: breaks down naturally through the action of bacteria
greenhouse gas: a gas that traps the air around the Earth, causing a rise in temperature
recycle: to process products so they can be used again

3.2: Environmental issues

133

Car crisis?

Sustainable transport

The European Union gives 50 million Euros to fund transport projects.

Berlin: State officials' cars and vans converted to natural gas. Can be used by private persons outside working hours, as part of a car-share scheme.

Graz (Austria): Bus fleet and taxis converted to diesel. Polluting vehicles pay more to park.

Bristol: A 'clean zone' in city centre. Reduced parking. Road pricing.

1 What is the aim of these projects?

2 Are these projects sustainable? Give reasons.

Rome: City promotes electric scooters. On-street recharging facilities. Better traffic lights reduce congestion and pollution.

The real cost of motoring

A car gives you the freedom to go where you like, when you like. But what is the real cost of motoring?

Over 200 new cars are sold every hour in the UK, and though newer cars have 'greener' engines, they still emit greenhouse gases. Road traffic is now a major cause of air pollution. Traffic fumes not only pollute our cities, they affect rural areas too.

Government figures predict that road traffic will increase by 75% in the next 30 years. As congestion nears gridlock in many towns and cities, the average UK motorist spends a total of five days a year just sitting in traffic jams. Many people say they would use public transport if it were cheaper, cleaner and safer.

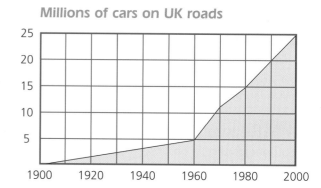

Millions of cars on UK roads

Source: www.statistics.gov.uk

You will investigate the range of problems created by traffic, and consider some sustainable solutions.

Possible solutions

Road pricing

Road users pay for using roads. Cars can be fitted with electronic number plates that give signals to special computers. The computer works out when the car was on a particular road and the driver is charged. In Singapore, this system has reduced rush-hour traffic, pollution and damage to roads. In London, people pay the congestion charge to drive their cars into the central area.

A drawback is that richer people can afford the charges, so poorer people could be disadvantaged.

Bike it!

The National Cycling Stategy in the UK aims to encourage people to cycle. The hope is to reduce pollution, improve local environments and people's health. Its work includes:

- providing more cycle routes so people can travel around easily and safely
- providing secure cycle parks at bus and train stations to make it convenient for people to use public transport for longer journeys
- encouraging train companies to provide spaces for bikes on trains.

Improving public transport

Better public transport might encourage people to stop using their cars so much. Possible plans are to:

- improve bus reliability
- decrease bus journey times
- develop tram systems
- reduce car traffic.

This could be done by:

- creating bus lanes on important routes and making sure cars don't use them
- giving priority at traffic lights to buses, pedestrians and cyclists
- stopping cars parking on busy routes.

Action

1 Research alternative forms of transport that might be used in towns and cities, such as electric powered cars. Do they offer sustainable alternatives to petrol/diesel driven vehicles?
2 How does road traffic affect the lives of people in your local area? What could be done to improve the situation?

Check your understanding

1 In what ways should public transport be improved to encourage more people to use it?
2 What are the advantages of the possible solutions to the car crisis? Are there disadvantages?

What's your opinion?

'Building more roads is the only solution to the UK's traffic problems.'
Do you agree with this statement? Give reasons for your opinion, showing you have considered another point of view.

Key Terms

road pricing: a scheme which charges road users according to how much they use a road

We all share the same air

Getting you thinking

"Pollution doesn't need a passport"

Chernobyl nuclear power station after the fire

After the Chernobyl nuclear power station fire in Russia, clouds of radioactive material were carried as far as the UK. Two years later, sheep on the Cumbrian fells were still being monitored for signs of radiation.

The River Danube rises in Germany, then flows through Austria, Hungary, Romania and Bulgaria before it reaches the Black Sea. So if pollution of the Danube is to be controlled effectively, then each of these countries has to be 'a good neighbour' to all the others.

1 Explain why pollution 'doesn't need a passport'.

2 What other ways can one country's action affect other countries' environments?

Climate change and global warming

Climate change is a complex subject that is not fully understood. Our climate is changing, but scientists disagree about why it is happening and what the long-term effects of these global changes will be.

Many influential scientists believe the burning of **fossil fuels** is responsible for **global warming**. The concentration of the main greenhouse gas, carbon dioxide (CO_2), in the atmosphere is now at its highest for 400 000 years, and global warming is taking place faster than expected. Temperatures are rising more quickly than at any time in the past 1000 years.

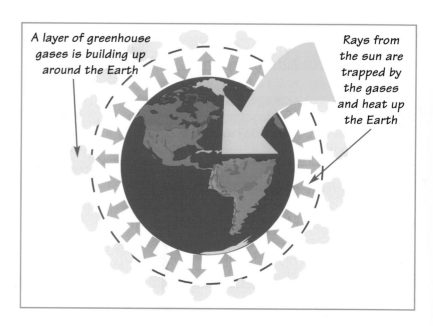

A layer of greenhouse gases is building up around the Earth

Rays from the sun are trapped by the gases and heat up the Earth

You will discover that all countries are interdependent because pollution and global warming are not contained within national boundaries.

What are the effects?

Climate changes can have both positive and negative effects. Higher levels of CO_2 in the atmosphere may improve crop yields, but they could also lead to water shortages.

There would be regional winners and losers from global warming. On balance, the LEDCs would suffer more than the MEDCs. There are already water shortages in countries such as Rwanda, Somalia and Kenya, and these are likely to get worse, bringing widespread crop failure and famine.

Rise in sea levels

As over half the world's population live on low-lying coastal plains and estuaries, millions of people could become environmental refugees.

Hurricanes, flooding and droughts

The possibility of more extreme weather threatens the livelihood of many of the poorest people in the world.

Richer nations, which produce the vast majority of greenhouse gases, will be affected by changes in weather patterns too. Violent storms and heavy rains hit some areas and drought affects others.

Disease

Warmer and wetter conditions in other areas will increase waterborne infections like malaria, diarrhoea and dysentery. Higher temperatures would mean a rise in the number of pests, weeds and diseases.

It might be necessary to increase pesticide and weedkiller use, which could lead to polluted rivers and lakes.

Over 10 000 people were washed away in floods in the Indian State of Orissa. Salt water ruined the crops and the land will take a long time to recover.

Action

1 Research the sources, both manufactured and natural, of greenhouse gas emissions. Use this information to suggest ways that emissions could be reduced in future.

2 Research which areas of the UK would be affected by rising sea levels. Which industries would be threatened by floods? How would local economies be affected? What, if anything, can government and/or local councils do to prepare for this?

Check your understanding

1 In your own words, explain what greenhouse gases are.
2 List some of the likely effects of global warming.
3 Why do you think the world's leading climate scientists now argue that all nations must cooperate to reduce emissions of these gases?

What's your opinion?

'Global warming's great. It means we have long hot summers.'
Do you agree with this statement? Give reasons for your opinion, showing you have considered another point of view.

Cutting carbon: the Kyoto Protocol

In 1998, world leaders met in Kyoto, Japan, to discuss how to reduce global emissions of greenhouse gases. They agreed to reduce emissions by an average of 5% below 1990 levels by the year 2008. Many scientists argued this wasn't enough and that it would need emission cuts of up to 60%.

Key Terms

fossil fuel: a naturally-occurring fuel, such as coal or natural gas

global warming: the rise in average surface temperature of the Earth

The European family

Getting you thinking

The European Union (EU) is a trading area. When countries sell things to each other, they often have to pay taxes on products before they are allowed into the other country. The EU removed these taxes between countries within the EU so that they could trade freely with each other.

In order to allow this trade to be as free as possible, rules have been drawn up about a range of things that affect how businesses work. The rules aim to make competition fairer between countries so they are all working on 'a level playing field'.

The rules are about:

Protecting employees
Without EU regulations, one country could allow children to work in factories. That country could make things more cheaply because wages would be lower.

Protecting the environment
If one country allowed businesses to pollute the environment, production would be cheaper because they wouldn't have to clean up the mess that was made.

Guaranteeing product standards
If a country is making poor-quality products, they may be dangerous.

Promoting fair competition
Businesses are not allowed to have too much power. For example, if a business controlled prices unfairly, this would hurt the customer.

1 Why do you think the European Union has rules like this?

2 If one country broke the rules, how might this affect other countries in the EU?

What is the European Union?

At the end of World War II in 1945, the countries of Europe were anxious that war should not break out again. By joining together more closely, it was felt that war would be less likely. Ever since 1958, more countries have become involved and have worked together ever closer in all sorts of areas, including economics, politics, the environment and social issues.

The European Union:

- promotes economic and social progress

- gives the EU a voice on the international scene

- introduces EU citizenship

- develops an area of freedom, security and justice

- maintains and establishes EU regulations.

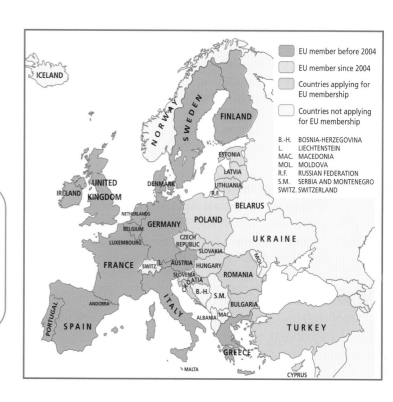

EU member before 2004

EU member since 2004

Countries applying for EU membership

Countries not applying for EU membership

B.-H. BOSNIA-HERZEGOVINA
L. LIECHTENSTEIN
MAC. MACEDONIA
MOL. MOLDOVA
R.F. RUSSIAN FEDERATION
S.M. SERBIA AND MONTENEGRO
SWITZ. SWITZERLAND

You will explore the structure of the European Union, what it does and how its power is distributed among its institutions.

How the EU works

All member countries, or **member states**, of the EU elect Members of the European Parliament (MEPs). MEPs have much bigger constituencies than MPs in each country because the European Parliament has to represent all the member countries: 380 million people in total. The European Parliament has 732 members altogether. The UK Parliament has 646 MPs compared with 78 MEPs.

The European Parliament is one of the five organizations that run the EU. It is, however, not quite like the UK Parliament, which has power to make laws. Look at the diagram below to decide where the power lies.

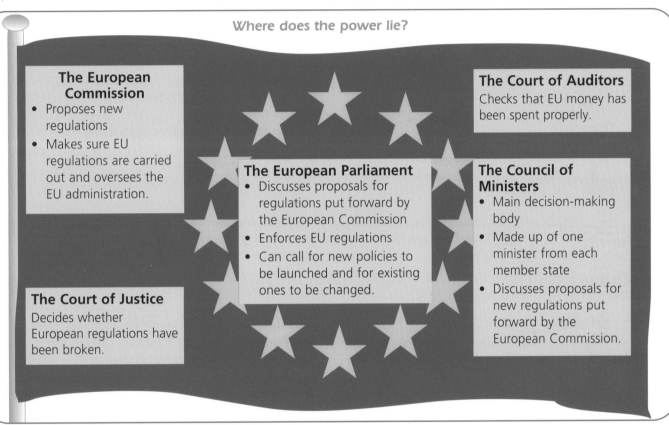

Where does the power lie?

The European Commission
- Proposes new regulations
- Makes sure EU regulations are carried out and oversees the EU administration.

The Court of Justice
Decides whether European regulations have been broken.

The European Parliament
- Discusses proposals for regulations put forward by the European Commission
- Enforces EU regulations
- Can call for new policies to be launched and for existing ones to be changed.

The Court of Auditors
Checks that EU money has been spent properly.

The Council of Ministers
- Main decision-making body
- Made up of one minister from each member state
- Discusses proposals for new regulations put forward by the European Commission.

Action
1 Which European constituency are you in?
2 Who is your MEP?
3 Which political party do they belong to?

Check your understanding
1 Which organization in the EU holds most power?
2 How is the EU different from the UK in this respect?
3 How democratic is decision-making in the EU compared with the UK?

What's your opinion?
'Countries that trade together should all have the same rules for running businesses.'
Do you agree with this statement? Give reasons for your opinion, showing you have considered another point of view.

Key Terms
member state: a country which is a member of the EU

Citizens of Europe

Getting you thinking

A bigger market

Herman Miller is an international business based in the USA. However, it makes office furniture in the UK, Germany and Italy and sells it throughout Europe. There is a lot of competition between businesses selling office furniture, so Herman Miller must keep its prices low and look after its customers. Being in the EU means that there are fewer forms to fill in and fewer delays when lorries cross the borders between European countries. There are also no taxes to pay when furniture is sold to other European countries. If it came from the USA, for example, there would be taxes to pay.

Because the furniture is manufactured in the EU, it means that both the materials that they need to make it and the finished products themselves can be delivered more quickly, reliably and cheaply.

1 Do you think that Herman Miller thinks the EU is a good or bad thing?

2 Why do you think Herman Miller wants to keep factories going in Europe?

3 How does the EU affect customers?

Inside or out?

The EU combines its member states into one big market. Businesses can sell their products in any EU state so there is lots of competition. This means that prices should be lower.

The downside is that things bought from countries outside the EU are more expensive. A tax, or **customs duty**, has to be paid on goods from other parts of the world, so these goods would probably cost more for an EU consumer.

These factors have meant that the UK buys and sells more products to EU countries than any other part of the world.

What about the Euro?

The **Euro** was set up on 1 January 1999. It is the **single currency** for some members of the EU.

When the Euro was launched, the UK decided not to join because, among other things, the UK economy was not in line with other European countries.

The Euro can make things more straightforward.

- People and businesses don't have to change money from one currency to another when they travel to different countries within the European Union. This makes things cheaper because banks charge for changing money.

- It makes things more certain. The value of currencies change against each other. If you go on holiday to the USA, the number of dollars you can buy with your pounds will change from day to day. If everyone in Europe uses the Euro, a business knows that there will be no change in the price it receives for products sold in other European Union countries.

Not everyone is in favour of the Euro. The main concern is that it reduces a country's control over its own economy. If a lot of people are unemployed, the government might want to use policies that help to create jobs. This might be difficult if these policies did not fit with EU policy.

You will investigate how business and citizenship in the UK is affected by European Union regulations.

Citizens of the European Union

Any citizen of a country within the EU is automatically an EU citizen. This does not interfere with your national rights but adds four special rights to them:

- **Freedom to move and take up residence anywhere in the Union**

You can get a job anywhere in the EU. It is much harder to get work in other parts of the world.

- **The right to vote and stand in local government and European Parliament elections in the country of residence**

A British citizen living in another member state could stand for election there.

- **The right for EU citizens to be protected by representatives of any member state in countries where an individual's country is not represented**

Wherever you are in the world, an EU representative can help you out if you are in difficulties.

- **The right of appeal to the European ombudsman**

If you feel that EU rulings have not been carried out properly, you can appeal to the **European ombudsman** to investigate.

Action

1 Collect as much information about the Euro as possible. Make a display, using the evidence you have collected, about how the Euro is affecting the UK.
2 What does European citizenship mean to people who you know?
3 Would they describe themselves as Europeans? Are there any situations when they would be more or less likely to call themselves Europeans?

Check your understanding

1 Give two reasons why it can be cheaper to buy goods from within the European Union than from outside it.
2 Why could belonging to the Euro be a problem for individual EU countries?
3 As a British citizen, would you be allowed to work in Spain? Give reasons.
4 If you were travelling outside the European Union and you needed help from officials, who could you go to if you found out there was no British embassy or representative in that area?

What's your opinion?

'I am a European.'
Do you agree with this statement? Give reasons for your opinion, showing you have considered another point of view.

Key Terms

customs duty: taxes on products bought from other countries

Euro: the name of the single currency used by a group of countries within the European Union (Belgium, Germany, Greece, Spain, France, Ireland, Italy, Luxembourg, the Netherlands, Austria, Portugal and Finland)

European ombudsman: a person who investigates complaints against the EU

single currency: this is the Euro, so called as it is used in some of the EU member states

The Commonwealth

Daily bread

Elizabeth Namwala, 29, is a mother living in Chipata Compound, a low-income housing estate in Lusaka, Zambia. Elizabeth used to sell four to five pans of bread a day.

She then received some loans from the Commonwealth Youth Credit Initiative. The money went towards buying stocks of ingredients. Now, Elizabeth sells 50 pans of bread a day. She repaid her first and second loans before the due date and is now repaying a third. Elizabeth has expanded her business and employs five young people. She has improved her house, and her living standards have risen.

1 Who gave Elizabeth her loan?

2 How did the loan help Elizabeth?

3 How did the loan help other people?

4 Why do you think the Commonwealth Youth Credit Initiative gives loans to people in developing countries?

The Commonwealth today

The **Commonwealth of Nations**, usually just called the Commonwealth, is an association of countries, most of which were ruled by Britain. However, today's Commonwealth is a world away from the handful of countries which were the first members. From Africa and Asia to the Pacific and the Caribbean, the Commonwealth's 1.7 billion people make up 30% of the world's population.

The modern Commonwealth helps to advance democracy, human rights and sustainable economic and social development within its member countries and beyond. Zimbabwe was thrown out of the Commonwealth in 2003 because it infringes human rights and its elections are not very democratic. All the countries have English as a common working language and similar systems of law, public administration and education. The Queen, just like her predecessors, is head of the Commonwealth. It has built on its shared history to become a vibrant and growing association of states.

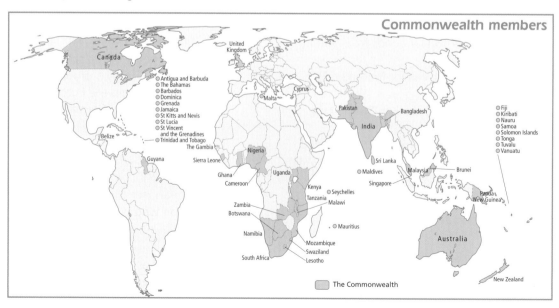

Commonwealth members

The Commonwealth

You will find out how the Commonwealth has changed from its origins, and the type of work it does today.

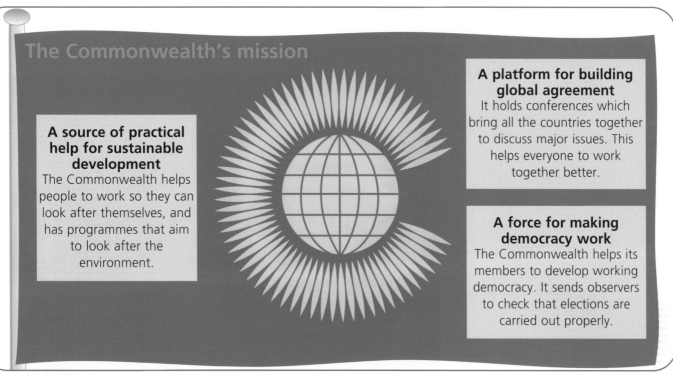

The Commonwealth's mission

A source of practical help for sustainable development
The Commonwealth helps people to work so they can look after themselves, and has programmes that aim to look after the environment.

A platform for building global agreement
It holds conferences which bring all the countries together to discuss major issues. This helps everyone to work together better.

A force for making democracy work
The Commonwealth helps its members to develop working democracy. It sends observers to check that elections are carried out properly.

How does it do its work?

The Commonwealth has all sorts of ways of helping people and encouraging them to work together. Here are two examples:

The Commonwealth Fund for Technical Cooperation (CFTC)

The CFTC promotes economic and social development, and helps to overcome poverty in member countries. The skills of member countries are used to help others. Advisors go to other countries to help in agriculture, enterprise, trade, legal issues, etc.

Action

1 Have any countries joined the Commonwealth recently?
2 What are the conditions for joining the Commonwealth?
3 Why do countries want to be members of the Commonwealth?
4 Find an example of a recent Commonwealth sustainable development programme and present your findings to the class.

Check your understanding

1 What are the origins of the Commonwealth?
2 How has it changed over the years?
3 What is its mission today?
4 Describe some ways in which it achieves its mission.

What's your opinion?

'The Commonwealth is the same as it has always been.'
Do you agree with this statement? Give reasons for your opinion, showing you have considered another point of view.

The Commonwealth Youth Credit Initiative (CYCI)

The CYCI is a small enterprise scheme for young people providing 'micro-credit' (small-scale lending), training and enterprise development. Low-cost, easily accessible credit and training can bring economic self-sufficiency to the poorest young people. The CYCI provides these services using the following methods:

- low interest rates
- low training costs
- use of young people to support each other, and to encourage saving and the paying back of loans
- ongoing training and monitoring of enterprises.

Key Terms

Commonwealth of Nations: a voluntary group of independent countries

A united world?

Getting you thinking

For generations, Kosovo has been fought over by Serbs and Albanians. Both peoples have centuries' old claims to the land.

For a decade they were at war with each other over control of the region. Finally, the United Nations stepped in to keep the peace. UN personnel dealt with law and order, health and education, and ensuring the safe return of **refugees** to their homes.

1 Why do you think the Serbs and Albanians needed help to bring the war to an end? What might have happened if it hadn't?

2 Why do you think refugees needed help to find their families and return home?

3 Why do you think people respect the soldiers from the UN?

The United Nations

Nearly every nation in the world belongs to the **United Nations**. Its membership totals 191 countries.

When states join, they agree to accept the UN charter. The aims of the charter are:

- to maintain international peace and security
- to develop friendly relations among nations
- to cooperate in solving international problems and in promoting respect for human rights
- to be a centre for harmonizing the actions of nations.

The UN is not a world government and it does not make laws. It does, however, help to resolve international conflict and makes policies on matters affecting us all. At the UN, all the member states have a voice and can vote in this process.

Peacekeeping: the work of the UN Security Council

The Security Council is made up of five permanent members, including the United Kingdom, and 15 non-permanent members who are elected for two years at a time. As the world changes, the number of permanent members may change.

The Security Council:

- can investigate any international dispute
- can recommend ways of reaching a settlement
- is responsible for peacekeeping forces.

You will explore the work of the United Nations and consider its role in the world.

An Afghan family enters Pakistan from Afghanistan to go to a refugee camp

Refugees

For more than five decades, the United Nations High Commission on Refugees has been helping the world's uprooted peoples.

The agency's first task was to help an estimated one million people after World War II. During the 1950s, the refugee crisis spread to Africa, Asia and then back to Europe. It had become a global problem.

During its lifetime the agency has assisted an estimated 50 million refugees to restart their lives.

Humanitarian action and human rights

Child soldiers in Africa are looked after by the UN and educated in order to help them to fit into society again. Often their families can't be found. This is just one of many projects to help people in difficulties.

"The soldiers gave me training. They gave me a gun. I took drugs. I killed civilians. Lots. It was just war, what I did then. I only took orders. I knew it was bad. It was not my wish."

Development and trade

The UN also aims to help developing countries grow and trade fairly with the rest of the world. It works to improve the standard of living by making recommendations and giving guidance on economic development.

Action

1 Research a current UN peacekeeping operation. Why are people fighting? How is the UN helping? Is it 'maintaining international peace and security'?
2 Find a recent example of work done by the UN High Commission on Refugees. Why had the refugees left home? How has the High Commission helped?

Check your understanding

1 What kind of work does the UN do?
2 Is the UN a government? Explain your answer.
3 Describe the Security Council's responsibilities.
4 Why is the UK important in the Security Council?
5 Why do you think the UN needs to intervene in the conflicts mentioned?
6 Why might the UN be able to help refugees more effectively than individual countries?
7 Which human rights are the child soldiers being denied?

What's your opinion?

'Countries should not be allowed to be members of the UN if their populations' human rights are not respected.'
Do you agree with this statement? Give reasons for your opinion, showing you have considered another point of view.

Key Terms

refugees: people who have been forced to leave their country and must live somewhere else

United Nations: an international organization that tries to encourage peace, cooperation and friendship between countries

3.3: The UK's place in the world

Global crisis: global action

Getting you thinking

HIV/AIDS: a global problem

1 Which continent has the highest rates of HIV/AIDS?

2 Suggest reasons for the difference between infection rates in Europe and sub-Saharan Africa.

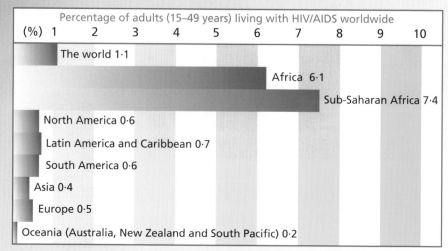

Percentage of adults (15–49 years) living with HIV/AIDS worldwide

(%) 1 2 3 4 5 6 7 8 9 10

The world 1·1

Africa 6·1

Sub-Saharan Africa 7·4

North America 0·6

Latin America and Caribbean 0·7

South America 0·6

Asia 0·4

Europe 0·5

Oceania (Australia, New Zealand and South Pacific) 0·2

Source: Population Reference Bureau 2004

Dying of ignorance

In the year 2000, the number of 10- to 19-year-olds on the planet reached one billion. Most of these young people live in LEDCs.

Half of all new **HIV** infection is occurring in young people. Because of a lack of even basic health education, many young people in LEDCs are unaware of the risks they face and don't know how to protect themselves. Poor countries can't afford to set up clinics, provide HIV testing or distribute free condoms.

UNICEF, an agency of the UN, estimates that one-half of today's 15-year-olds in Botswana and South Africa will die from **AIDS**.

UNAIDS: the UN and the World Health Organization at work

The United Nations works with many other organizations worldwide to fight the spread of HIV/AIDS. In 1987, it set up a special global programme to deal with the problem. Since 1996, this programme has been run by UNAIDS, with the help of 30 other UN organizations, such as the World Health Organization (WHO) and UNICEF.

UNAIDS' role is to help governments to help themselves, and not to impose a 'UN solution' on a local problem.

Here are some examples of projects that have been supported by UNAIDS.

UNAIDS teamed up with MTV to promote HIV/AIDS awareness to its one billion viewers around the world.

UNAIDS worked with the Ministry of Health in Brazil on a project which targeted 100 000 'at-risk' teenagers and 80 000 injecting drug users.

UNAIDS sponsored the TV soap 'I Need to Know', which goes out on 20 television stations across Nigeria. The programme tries to persuade viewers that 'silence can be deadly', and encourages young people to speak out about taboo topics such as HIV/AIDS.

UNAIDS works with local agencies in southern Africa on a project aimed at preventing HIV/AIDS infection, particularly in adolescent girls.

UNAIDS collaborates with local churches in Chikankata, Zambia, helping to care for 1500 'AIDS orphans' from local villages.

1 Why did UNAIDS team up with MTV?

2 Why did the Brazilian government target teenagers and injecting drug users? What other groups might have been targeted?

3 Give reasons why UNAIDS used a TV soap to get health messages across in Nigeria.

4 Why does UNAIDS think it is important to support local programmes?

You will explore the impact of HIV/AIDS and the work the United Nations does to combat this epidemic.

Wake up to HIV/AIDS

Kindlimuka, which means 'wake up', is Mozambique's first self-help group for people living with HIV/AIDS. UNICEF supports the group.

Over 20 million people in Mozambique are HIV positive, with some 600 new infections every day. Of the new infections, 45% of new sufferers are under the age of 25. Most do not know they are infected.

Kindlimuka works with local schoolchildren. The director, Adriano Matsinhe, says, "Because I look healthy, the children think I'm paid to say I'm HIV-positive."

Matsinhe is one of the few people in Mozambique who has openly admitted he is HIV-positive on television. The stigma of HIV/AIDS is one of the greatest challenges sufferers have to face, and Kindlimuka has been a breakthrough. It's a real community service. Many families now visit the centre.

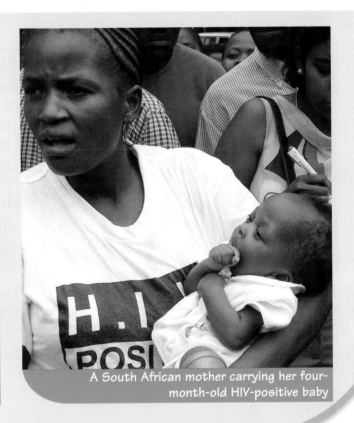

A South African mother carrying her four-month-old HIV-positive baby

Action

1. Using organizations such as the Terence Higgins Trust, research rates of HIV infection in the UK and the support available to those infected.
2. Compare UK rates and support with information for another region of the world.
3. HIV/AIDS will have long-term economic effects in LEDCs, such as Mozambique. In groups, discuss how the epidemic might affect the following in a poor country:
- family earnings
- food supplies
- education levels
- health services.

Check your understanding

1. Why are so many young people in LEDCs 'dying of ignorance'?
2. HIV/AIDS is a global problem, but why is it a more urgent problem in Africa than in Europe?
3. Why do you think the Mozambique project is called 'wake up'?
4. In your own words, what is the main challenge faced by AIDS workers such as Adriano Matsinhe?

What's your opinion?

'Raising awareness of HIV/AIDS is the most important thing to do when dealing with the disease.'

Do you agree with this statement? Give reasons for your opinion, showing you have considered another point of view.

Key Terms

AIDS: acquired immune deficiency syndrome, a disease that destroys people's natural defences against diseases

HIV: human immunodeficiency virus, a virus that reduces people's resistance to illness and can cause AIDS

A louder voice

Getting you thinking

1 Why are people tortured?

2 How many countries use torture?

3 Why is it wrong?

4 How do you think you can help Amnesty International to end torture?

TORTURE is wrong, unjust and it should never happen to anyone

EVERYONE has the right not to be tortured. Everyone also has the right to be free of the threat of torture. But in the world in which we live, many people are tortured. In fact, in more than 150 countries, torture is used to hurt, frighten and punish people.

This booklet is about torture and what you can do to stop torture. It has been written by an organization called Amnesty International. Please help us to make the world free of torture.
Stop Torture

International pressure groups

There are several international pressure groups campaigning across the world. Two of the most well known international pressure groups are Amnesty International and Greenpeace. Amnesty International campaigns to save people who are imprisoned, hurt or threatened by the government of a country. It promotes the values of the Universal Declaration of Human Rights. Greenpeace campaigns on environmental issues, and works to protect the Earth from environmental threats such as global warming, pollution and the use of nuclear power.

How does Amnesty International work?

Amnesty International has around one million members and supporters in 162 countries. Activities range from public demonstrations to letter writing, from human rights education to fundraising concerts, from individual appeals on a particular case to global campaigns on a particular issue.

Amnesty International is impartial and independent of any government or religion. Like many other pressure groups, it is run by its members. Its aim is to put pressure on governments and other organizations to change the way they behave. By joining together, people can have a greater effect.

Amnesty uses the power of the individual to put on the pressure. The organization publicizes human rights abuses and asks its members to write to the relevant governments or authorities in protest. One letter would have little effect but hundreds or thousands might make people listen. These are the sorts of strategies used by many large pressure groups.

Other ways of campaigning

Pressure groups work in many different ways. Like Amnesty International, Greenpeace often encourages people to send a message. It supplies e-cards that can be emailed to anyone.

It also campaigns in other ways:

- it has sent ships to places where the environment is under threat
- it has anchored ships where a country was carrying out nuclear tests
- activists have boarded an oil platform which was to be sunk with the threat of pollution.

Greenpeace's actions are sometimes outside the law, but the organization feels very strongly that these methods are the most effective way of getting people to listen.

You will understand how individuals can work with international organizations to help bring about change in the world.

Eritrea
Prisoner of conscience

Mother of four Aster Yohannes was detained by security personnel in December 2003 when she returned to Eritrea to be with her children after three years of study in the USA. Amnesty International believes she is detained solely because of her husband's political opinions.

Her husband, prisoner of conscience Petros Solomon, was head of security and intelligence in the Eritrean People's Liberation Front (EPLF) during the liberation struggle.

Please write, calling for the immediate and unconditional release of prisoners of conscience Aster Yohannes and her husband Petros Solomon. Call for Aster Yohannes to be given immediate access to any necessary medical care.

Source: www.amnesty.org

Action

1 Is there an Amnesty International or Greenpeace local action group in your area? Interview members of the group and find out what they do.
2 Choose an international pressure group and find out how it works. What are its successes? How did they happen? Present your findings to the class.

Check your understanding

1 What is the main focus of Amnesty International's work?
2 How can individuals join in Amnesty International's campaigns?
3 Why is group pressure more effective than individual pressure?
4 Describe the effect Greenpeace can have on large corporations.

What's your opinion?

Pressure groups always try to improve things for everyone.'
Do you agree with this statement? Give reasons for your opinion, showing you have considered another point of view.

A letter on the Greenpeace website

I work for a big company and I have to tell you that Greenpeace's tactics do make an impression and have impact. In this age of 'spin' and image consciousness, the last thing most companies want is visible, messy, physical confrontation. The mere existence of Greenpeace (and other activist groups) and the threat of embarrassing media coverage puts a check on bad corporate behaviour. Even if they deny this, it is always in the back of their mind. Your work, and especially your high profile activities, help us keep the business people from getting completely out of control.
So, don't change, don't become more mainstream, don't smooth off the rough edges, and don't dumb-down to mediocrity. Insiders like me need your visibility and activism!

Source: Greenpeace www.greenpeace.org

Greenpeace activists boarding an oil platform to prevent it being sunk

The global village: the exam

Evidence-based questions

Use the source and your own knowledge.

Rights and Responsibilities for Global Multinationals

Multinational companies like Adidas and Sony make their products world-wide. They benefit from low wages and cheap materials to sell products round the world. Local workers get jobs they would not have otherwise had – so they are better off too. Also, the shareholders receive more profits than they would have had if the trainers, sports clothing or electrical goods had been made in the UK, USA or Japan.

Some multinationals such as Unilever adopt ethical policies to put back benefits into the poor countries where they work. They take their responsibilities seriously. In many communities, the health and living standards of local people have been improved by Unilever's community programmes which provide water, hygiene and education.

In complete contrast, the campaigning group Christian Aid criticises some big companies. It says British American Tobacco claims to provide local farmers with necessary training and protective clothing – but farmers in Kenya and Brazil say this does not happen. Christian aid also criticises Coca Cola. In India, one of its companies is accused of empting village wells in an area where water in scarce. The company has been told by an Indian court to stop taking the water.

Source: adapted from www.greenwichgateway.com and christian-aid.org.uk

1. Paragraph 1 refers to shareholders of multinational companies. Put a cross in the box *(2 marks)* that indicates the right answer.

   i) What is a shareholder?
   A shareholder:
   A   is someone who is employed by and shares the aims of the country ☐
   B   owns shares in the company and receives a share of the profit ☑
   C   is someone who sells a share of his produce to the company ☐

   ii) What is a multinational company? Put a cross in the box which indicates the correct answer.
   A multinational company is called multinational because:
   A   it conducts its business in many different countries ☑
   B   it employs people with ethnic minority backgrounds ☐
   C   it has people from different countries on its board of directors ☐

2. Look at paragraph 1. How do local people benefit when multinational companies *(1 mark)* start making their products in less economically developed countries?
   Multinational companies provide jobs for local people so they are better off than they might have been.

Leave margin blank

150

3. Give and explain one example of a multinational taking its responsibilities seriously. *(2 marks)*

Unilever takes it responsibilities seriously. It has community programmes which provide clean water, hygiene and education to improve people's health and way of life.

4. Give and explain one example of a multinational company which, it is suggested, may *(2 marks)* not be behaving responsibly.

British American Tobacco claimed to be providing training and protective clothing for its workers, but Christian Aid claimed that it wasn't.

5. Use the source and your own knowledge. Give and explain one reason why national governments find it difficult to control multinational companies.

Multinational companies work in many countries so it is hard for any one country to control them. Because they are often looking for cheaper ways of making things, they may move from one country to another when laws are tightened to protect workers and the environment.

> You might also have used Coca Cola as an example. It has been draining wells to make Coca Cola in one of its factories in India. A local court has told it to stop.

> This question asks you to use your own knowledge as well as the information in the passage. You can only get full marks by adding some of the information you have learnt during your Citizenship Studies course.

Leave margin blank

Source: Edexcel Citizenship Studies 2005

Short answer questions

1. Boxes A, B and C describe three important parts of the European Union *(3 marks)*

Box A	Box B	Box C
The decision making body; makes EU laws	It suggests changes to EU policy; makes sure EU laws are carried out and oversees EU administration	It exercises democratic control and is the body which decides the EU budget

i.   Which box describes the Council of Ministers?
Box A

ii.   Which box describes the European Parliament?
Box C

iii. Which box describes the European Commission?
Box B

> You might have thought that the Parliament should be the main decision-making body, so try to remember that it's the council of Ministers that makes the decisions.

2. Explain one difference between the Commonwealth and the United Nations. *(2 marks)*

The Commonwealth is mainly made up of countries which used to be ruled by Britain. The UN is made up of countries which want to encourage human rights, peace keeping, combating poverty and helping to make people's lives better.

3. Give one reason why some people believe wind farms should be established. *(1 mark)*

Wind farms help the environment because they provide sustainable energy.

4. Give one reason why some people are against building wind farms where they live. *(1 mark)*

People often don't want wind farms near where they live because they can be noisy and spoil the view.

5. Briefly explain one reason why it is sometimes suggested that the debts of LEDCs (less economically developed countries) should be cancelled. *(2 marks)*

When countries have big debts, they have to pay a lot of interest. This means that they have less money to spend on education, health and other things their populations need. Cancelling debts will make people's lives much better if the money is used to help a country's population.

6. Identify and explain one way in which the pattern of global trade could be made fairer. *(2 marks)*

Fair Trade schemes, such as Café Direct, which offer farmers a better return for their crops, can help to make global trade fairer. If the farmers are earning more money, they will have a better standard of living.

> If the richer countries of the world didn't have taxes, or tariffs, on imports from LEDCs, trade would also be fairer.

Source: Edexcel Citizenship Studies 2003, 2004, 2005

Extended writing

'Britain is never justified in going to war.' *(9 marks)*

Do you agree with this view?

Give reasons for your opinion, showing you have considered another point of view.

You could include some of the following points in your answer and other information of your own. You should support your points with examples, wherever possible.

• Should Britain take part in wars against terrorism?

• Should it go to war to enforce United Nations resolutions, eg Iraq?

• Should it help to free people from oppression?

• Who should try to keep the peace in civil wars?

• What is the role of public opinion and protest?

Source: Edexcel Citizenship Studies 2004

Wars happen for all sorts of reasons so it makes it hard to say that the country should never go to war. I can understand why people say we should never go to war because so many people are killed and badly injured, but a war might stop even more people being hurt.

> A great start! The student has looked at more than one point of view in the first paragraph.

Terrorism often hurts innocent people so it might be important to fight to prevent it. You should always think about what might happen if you go ahead too. Will a war really stop it or will it just make things worse? Perhaps it's more important to get people to talk instead of fighting. In Ireland people have started talking instead of fighting.

> Using examples is important and helps increase the number of marks you get, because it shows you understand the issues.

In some countries the ruler doesn't really care about the people in the country but just wants to stay in power. Mr Mugabe in Zimbabwe is an example of this. Some people think that we should sort things out because the people are suffering.

In some countries civil wars go on for years and years and in the end the United Nations steps in to help keep the peace, like it did in Serbia and Croatia. It is better to try to keep the peace while the two sides talk to each other. Joining in on one side or the other might just make things worse. The people in the country have to end up living together so it's better to talk about the problems.

> The student is working through the bullet points and each paragraph shows at least one point of view and additional ideas showing use of knowledge from the course.

We live in a democracy so the government should take notice of what the people think. We elect our MPs who decide which way to vote. Sometimes this doesn't seem to be enough and there are big demonstrations. This can persuade the government to change its mind but sometimes the protesters don't think they have much effect. At least it lets people know what you think.

> This shows that the student has a good understanding of the course as a whole, as it makes the link between democratic decision making and the question.

I don't think we should go to war unless there are very good reasons. Sometimes it is important to defend the country from attack, but I think we should talk about things first if it is possible. Whatever happens, it is important that the government thinks about what will happen as a result.

> The last paragraph gives a conclusion which is justified and draws on the rest of the answer.

Leave margin blank

Edexcel Ltd. accepts no responsibility whatsoever for the accuracy or method of working in the answers given.

153

Glossary

accountable: if you are accountable for something, you are responsible for it and have to explain your actions

Act: a law passed by Parliament

AIDS: acquired immune deficiency syndrome, a disease that destroys people's natural defences against diseases

appeal: a request for a decision made by a court to be reviewed

Assembly: a body of elected people to decide on some areas of spending in a region

barrister: a lawyer who represents and speaks for their clients in court

bias: to favour one thing over another unfairly

bill: a proposal to change something into law

biodegradable: breaks down naturally through the action of bacteria

boycott: to refuse to use or have anything to do with something

British national: citizen or subject of the United Kingdom

budget: the process each year when the Chancellor of the Exchequer explains how the government will raise and spend its money

business rates: a form of tax paid by all the businesses in an area. The amount a business pays depends on the rent that could be charged for their premises

cabinet: the main decision-making body of the council; also, a group of MPs who head major government departments. It meets weekly to make decisions about how government policy will be carried out

canvassing: when people try to persuade others to vote for their party in an election

censorship: limiting the information given to the general public

Chancellor of the Exchequer: the member of the government who is responsible for the country's finances

Chief Executive: an employee of the council, responsible for the smooth running of services

Citizens Advice Bureau (CAB): an organization that offers free advice on consumer and other legal matters

civil law: this covers disputes between individuals or groups. Civil law cases are often about rights between people

Commonwealth of Nations: a voluntary group of independent countries

community: a group of people in close contact and who share common interests and values

community sentence: when someone who has been convicted of a crime works in the community (clearing litter, for example) rather than going to prison

compensation: making amends for something; something given to make good a loss

constituency: the area represented by an MP

consumer: a person who buys goods or services for their own needs

contract of employment: a document which details an employee's and employer's responsibilities for a particular job

Convention: an agreement (often between governments)

council: a group of people who are elected to look after the affairs of a town, district or county

councillor: a member of a local council, elected by people in that area

council tax: a tax paid by everyone who lives in an area. It is based on the value of their house

county court: a local court that has limited powers in civil cases

criminal law: this deals with offences such as murder and drug dealing. These cases are between the Crown Prosecution Service (acting for all citizens) and the offender

crown court: courts held in towns in England and Wales where judges hear cases

cultural diversity: the range of different groups that make up a wider population

customs duty: taxes on products bought from other countries

Data Protection Act: a law that limits the way that information stored on computers can be used

Declaration: a document setting down aims and intentions

devolution: the transfer of power from central government to regional government

discrimination (racial, sex and disability): when a person is treated less favourably because of their colour, ethnic origins, gender or disability

dismissal: when employers end an employee's contract of employment (sometimes called 'sacking')

division of labour: where employees concentrate on a particular task or job at which they are expert

dual heritage: people with parents or ancestors of different origins

economic growth: this happens when the country produces more goods and services from year to year

economy: this is made up of all the organizations that provide goods and services, and all the individuals and organizations that buy them

editor: the person who is responsible for the content of a newspaper or television or radio programme

election: selection of one or more people for an official position by voting

electorate: all those registered to vote

emigration: leaving your homeland to live in another country

employment laws: laws passed by Parliament and by the European Union law-making bodies that set out the rights and responsibilities of employers and employees

employment tribunal: a type of court dealing only with disagreements over employment laws

Euro: the name of the single currency used by a group of countries within the European Union (Austria, Belgium, Finland, France, Germany, Greece, Ireland, Italy, Luxembourg, the Netherlands, Portugal and Spain)

European ombudsman: a person who investigates complaints against the EU

European Union: a group of 25 countries that works together fields such as the environment, social issues, the economy and trade

fair trade: a way of buying and selling products that aims to pay the producer a fair price

first past the post: an electoral system where voters have one vote per constituency and the candidate with the most votes wins

Forward Plan: a document which sets out the aims of the council in the long term

fossil fuel: a naturally-occurring fuel, such as coal or natural gas

Freedom of Information Act: a law which gives open access to information about individuals, business and government

free trade: trade between countries which is restricted by things like high taxes on imports

general election: an election for a new government. In the UK, these take place at least every five years

globalization: the increasing interdependence of the world

global warming: the rise in average surface temperature of the Earth

government revenue: the money raised by the government

greenhouse gas: a gas that traps the air around the Earth, causing a rise in temperature

Green Paper: this puts forward ideas that the government wants discussed before it starts to develop a policy

hereditary peers: people who inherited the title 'Lord' or 'Lady'

High Court: the highest court where judges hear cases on serious crimes

HIV: human immunodeficiency virus, a virus that reduces people's resistance to illness and can cause AIDS

homophobic: having a fear or hatred of homosexuals

House of Commons: the more powerful of the two parts of the British Parliament. Its members are elected by the public

human rights: things that people are morally or legally allowed to do or have

identity: who or what someone or something is

identity card: a card that establishes someone's identity

immigration: moving to another country to live there

inclusive education: schooling that involves everyone, regardless of disability or non-disability

industrial tribunal: a court dealing only with disagreements over employment laws

inflation: the general rise in prices

interdependent: where businesses need each other to survive

interest: extra payment paid to a lender by someone who has borrowed some money

journalist: a person who gathers news and produces reports for the media

judge: a person who decides questions of law in a court

judiciary: all the judges in a country

jury: a group of people who decide if someone is guilty in a court of law

LEDC: a less economically developed country

legal right: a right which is protected by law

libel: writing incorrect things about people

lobby: to try to persuade MPs to support a particular point of view. This used to happen in the 'lobby', or hallway, on the way into Parliament

ocal Agenda 21: a global plan to ask local eople how they think their immediate nvironment could be improved

gistrate: a public officer who deals with civil ases

gistrates' court: a court held before two or ore public officers dealing with minor crimes

ajority: the party with a majority has won a bigger proportion of the votes than the others

manifesto: a published statement of the aims and policies of a political party

mayor: a member of the council who is selected to be its representative on ceremonial occasions. In some areas they are the elected leader

MEDC: a more economically developed country

media: ways of communicating with large numbers of people

Member of Parliament: a person who has been elected to represent a constituency in Parliament

member state: a country which is a member of the EU

Minister of State: an assistant to the Secretary of State

minority: a small part of a larger group of people

minutes: a formal record of what has been said at a meeting

mitigating: making something less intense or severe

multicultural community: a community made up of people from many different cultural or ethnic groups

neighbourhood: a local area within which people live as neighbours, sharing living space and interests

Office of Fair Trading: a government office which can take action against traders who break the law

ombudsman: a person who investigates complaints against the government or a public organization

opinion poll: questioning a sample of the population to build a picture of the views of the public on a particular topic

opposition: political parties who are not in power

people's peers: people who are selected to sit in the House of Lords

political party: an organized group of people with common aims who put up candidates up for elections

polling station: a place where votes are cast; often a school, library or village hall

postal vote: when voters make their vote by post, rather than by going to a polling station

poverty line: the income level below which someone cannot afford to live

Press Code: guidelines for the media and journalists about the information they gather and how they obtain and use it

press freedom: the ability of the press to give information and express opinions without control

pressure group: a group of people who try to change public opinion or government policy to their own views or beliefs

Prime Minister: the leader of the majority party in the House of Commons and the leader of the government

private sector: this section of the economy is made up of businesses or organizations that are owned by individuals or by shareholders

probation officer: someone who writes court reports on offenders and supervises them in the community

profit: the money that you gain when you sell something for more than you paid for it or than it cost to make

proportional representation: an electoral system in which the number of seats a party wins is roughly proportional to its national share of the vote

public sector: this is made up of organizations owned or run by the government and local councils

racism: the idea that some people of different origins are not as good as others

rate of inflation: the rate at which prices rise

recorder: a barrister or solicitor of at least 10 years' experience who acts as a part-time judge in a crown court

recycle: to process products so they can be used again

redistributing income: taking money from wealthier people through taxation, to give it to poorer people through benefits

redundancy: when a person loses their job because the job doesn't need to be done anymore

redundant: losing your job because the job has ceased to exist

referendum: a vote by the whole electorate on a particular issue

refugees: people who have been forced to leave their country and must live somewhere else

rehabilitation: restoring a person to normal life

renewable: able to be replaced or restored

representative democracy: a type of democracy where citizens have the right to choose someone to represent them on a council or in Parliament as an MP

respect: to have a good opinion of someone

responsibility: something it is your duty to do or to look after

retraining: learning new skills that can be used in a different job

road pricing: a scheme which charges road users according to how much they use a road

school council: a group of people who represent the classes and year groups of the school. They give students the opportunity to participate in decision making

Secretary of State: an MP who is in charge of a government department such as health or defence

Shadow Cabinet: MPs from the main opposition party who 'shadow' MPs who head major government departments

shareholder: someone who owns part of a company by holding shares in that company

single currency: this is the Euro, so called as it is used in some of the EU member states

slander: saying incorrect things about people

small claims court: a local court, which hears civil cases involving small amounts of money

solicitor: a lawyer who gives legal advice and may speak for their clients in court

Speaker: the MP elected to act as Chairman for debates in the House of Commons

specialized: where employees or businesses concentrate on tasks that they can do well

spin doctor: someone who tries to get certain stories into the public eye and to make bad news sound better

stakeholder: someone who has an interest in a decision that is being made

sue: to make a claim against someone or something

sustainable development: living now in a way that doesn't damage the needs of future generations

tolerant: open-minded, accepting

trade unions: organizations that look after the interests of a group of employees

Trading Standards Department: an official body that enforces consumer-based laws

United Nations: an international organization that tries to encourage peace, cooperation and friendship between countries

ward: an area that forms a separate part of a local council

warning: written or spoken warning given by an employer to an employee if the employer thinks the employee has been breaking the contract of employment

White Paper: this puts government policy up for discussion before it becomes law

youth council: a group of young people who meet to discuss what is going on in the local area and put their ideas to the council